THE ULTIMATE GUIDE TO
TREES

THE ULTIMATE GUIDE TO
TREES

Jenny Linford

Bath · New York · Singapore · Hong Kong · Cologne · Delhi
Melbourne · Amsterdam · Johannesburg · Auckland · Shenzhen

This edition published by Parragon in 2011

Parragon
Queen Street House
4 Queen Street
Bath, BA1 1HE, UK
www.parragon.com

Produced by Atlantic Publishing

See page 256 for
photograph copyright details
Text © Parragon Books Ltd 2007
Cover design by Parragon & Ummagumma

ISBN 978-1-4454-5404-7
Printed in China

CONTENTS

CONIFERS AND MAIDENHAIR 30–69

FLOWERING TREES
PRIMITIVE ANGIOSPERMS 70–89

MONOCOTYLEDONS 90–111

DICOTYLEDONS 112–241

INTRODUCTION

Although trees are astonishingly diverse, existing in many different orders and families, there is a fundamental, underlying botany that unites them. A tree is typically characterised as a self-supporting, perennial plant, capable of reaching 6m (21ft) in height, which has a single woody stem (commonly known as a trunk), roots and branches that grow from year to year.

The first tree evolved over 370 million years ago in the form of Archaeopteris, complete with a woody trunk, branches that attached themselves to the trunk in the same way as a modern tree's do, and a root system. The arrival of Archaeopteris as a widespread plant form played a critical part in the Earth's developing ecosystem, filtering out the high levels of carbon dioxide present in the atmosphere at that time and creating conditions in which new land animals could evolve. Throughout the subsequent eras, trees continued to thrive and evolve. Conifers, tree ferns and ginkgo trees appeared during the Triassic era (245–208 million years ago). Many of today's trees first grew during the Tertiary era (65–2 million years ago). Trees continue to be highly successful life forms on our planet.

The trunk or woody stem, a defining characteristic of a tree, forms around 60 per cent of the total mass of any tree. A tree's trunk is key to its success as a plant, allowing it vital access to light, which the tree turns into food through a process called photosynthesis. The higher the tree can bring its leaves, the less competition for light there will be. The trunk, together with the branches, is part of a tree's internal transport system. The trunk and branches bring water, collected

Opposite: A magnificent Linden tree – the Common Lime (Tilea euopaea) – in autumn. When it flowers in spring, the perfume fills the air.

*Above: The Cork Oak (*Quercus suber*) has thick, spongy bark from which cork is made. Remarkably, the cork oak can withstand major stripping of its bark, simply renewing it within a few years.*
*Opposite below: America's Swamp Cypress (*Taxodium distichum*) has aerial roots known as 'knees'.*

by the roots, to the leaves. They also move food, produced by the leaves, to the other parts of the tree, including the roots. Incredibly, the only living cells in a tree's trunk and branches are in the area just beneath the tough outer waterproof bark. This fact explains how a tree can have a hollow trunk, as many ancient trees do, and yet continue to survive, and also how trees can be killed by ring-barking.

Although leaves vary hugely in appearance, from slender pine needles to large palm fronds, they all perform the same function. Leaves are the tree's food factory, the means by which the tree creates food for living and growing. Leaves contain chlorophyll, a green pigment, which absorbs light energy from the sun. This energy is then turned by the leaves into food for the tree in a process called photosynthesis, during which the leaves absorb carbon dioxide, transforming it into carbohydrates to feed the tree, and emit the waste product, oxygen. A tree's branches, which extend from the tree, allow its leaves to form a canopy and reach the most light possible, which can then be transformed into food for the tree.

A tree's root system makes up around 20 per cent of a its mass, as do a its branches. Roots function, of course, as an anchor for the tree's tall structure, connecting the tree to the ground. Roots, however, also work for the tree, drawing moisture and minerals from the ground. The first root that a tree grows from its seed is called the taproot, from which side roots or laterals grow. Despite the great heights that trees can grow to, most trees are comparatively shallow-rooted, with their roots found within 60–24cm (24–90in) of the surface; this, of course, makes them susceptible to being blown over in storms. While tree roots don't penetrate very deep into the ground, they do spread out considerably to form a wide radius around the trunk, becoming finer and finer the further away they are and sometimes spreading out to form a radius twice as large as the visible crown on top of the tree. Beneath the ground in a forest, therefore, competition for root space between the trees is intense.

Around the planet, different tree species have evolved different types of roots to suit the environment in which they grow. Rainforest trees are especially shallow-rooted, to make the most of the nutrients in the upper surface of the soil before they are washed away, and consequently they have what are known as 'buttress roots', which grow around the trunk above the ground and shore up the tree, exactly as a buttress on a cathedral does. Certain trees have adapted to growing in waterlogged conditions – for instance, America's Swamp Cypress produces aerial roots known as 'knees', which offer the tree vital access to oxygen.

Mangrove trees successfully live in salty water by developing prop roots (which grow from their trunks) and drop roots (which grow from their branches). These roots collect the oxygen that is needed to desalinate the water before it is sent through the tree's system. Certain trees, including the Weeping Fig, have developed what are known as pillar roots, which are very fast-growing roots that the tree sends down from its branches into the ground, where they root and form pillar-like supports for the tree. Ancient Banyan trees, which have these pillar roots, can cover a large area of ground, and often resemble a forest rather than a single tree.

IDENTIFICATION

Next time you go for a walk, look at the trees that you pass in gardens, parks, commons or fields and see how many you can recognise. We live surrounded by so many different species of tree and most of us only know how to identify a handful of them. Learning how to distinguish trees is a very satisfying process although, given how widely they can vary in appearance and how many different trees there are, learning to recognise them may seem a daunting task. Each tree, however, has a number of defining physical characteristics that are a genuine aid to identification: leaves, bark, flowers, fruit, buds and shape. When attempting to identify creatures such as birds or butterflies we can also take into account the range of the species. While this is often of help when trying to identify trees, because of their value to man as a source of food and other raw materials, many trees have become established in areas well beyond their natural distribution. The maps in this book give an indication of the natural distribution of the various species, or so far as can be ascertained, their place of origin.

*Above: The spiky leaves of the Holly (*Ilex aquifolium*) are quite distinctive.*
*Opposite: Australia's Blue Gum (*Eucalyptus globulus*) planted to dry out swampy land, particularly in central Africa, Italy and Turkey.*

A systematic approach, involving categorisation and elimination, can prove very rewarding and it is a real thrill when you do manage to correctly identify a tree. Tools that can aid the identification process include: a magnifying glass, for detailed examination of leaves and bark; binoculars, for closely examining leaves or cones that may be too high up to see clearly from the ground; a camera or notepad and coloured pencils, to record details such as height, size, shape and habitat and make sketches. Bark rubbings, done with wax crayons, are another useful record, and collecting leaf samples is a simple yet effective procedure.

Using leaves for identification

Leaves are enormously useful when it comes to identifying trees. One fundamental starting point is does the tree in question lose its leaves in the autumn or retain them all year round? If the former, then the tree is deciduous; if the latter, then it is evergreen.

What is the shape of the leaf? Leaf shapes vary greatly from straight, known as 'linear', to heart-shaped or rounded through to deeply lobed. Are the leaves fine needles or are they broad and flat? If broad and flat, are they what is known as compound leaves – that is divided into individual leaflets but growing from a single

leaf bud? If they are compound, then how are they arranged? Pinnate leaflets (e.g. Rowan) grow off a central stalk, either opposite each other in pairs or alternately. Palmate leaflets (e.g. Horse Chestnut), as their name suggests, grow at the end of a stalk and resemble a hand. The edges of a leaf, known botanically as 'margins', also vary in appearance. Smooth-edged leaves are known as 'entire', while leaves with serrated margins are 'toothed'. When the leaf is deeply indented it is known as 'lobed'. Leaf margins may also be wavy. The texture of a tree's leaves is another characteristic to be aware of. Are they fine or leathery? Rough, dull or glossy? Smooth or hairy? The size of a leaf is yet another factor, and leaf colours, range from many shades of green to silvery grey. The Copper Beech, for instance, is easily identified by its very striking and unusual purple-red foliage.

Above: The Oak (Quercus robur) has deeply indented lobed leaves.
Opposite: The Baobab (Adansonia digitata) can live for many centuries.

Using bark for identification

Very often the bark of a tree will change as it ages, characteristically changing from smooth to rough or fissured. Nonetheless, observing tree bark is a very useful aid to successful identification – especially so in winter when trying to distinguish between deciduous trees that have lost their leaves. An English Oak tree's bark, for example, with its vertical fissures, is very different from that of the Common Beech, which is silvery grey and smooth even in maturity. Key factors to note are the colour of the bark and its texture; certain cherry trees, for example, can be easily identified by their glossy, colourful bark, characteristically banded with

*Above: The Flowering Cherry (*Prunus serrulata*)
has pretty pink blossom in spring.
Opposite: Apples instantly identify the Cultivated
Apple (*Malus domestica*), although it comes in
many varieties.*

rough lenticels (raised breathing pores). The London Plane tree has distinctive bark because it peels off in layers, revealing cream-coloured patches of new bark beneath.

Using flowers for identification

If the tree you are trying to identify is in flower, this can be a great aid to recognition. Horse Chestnuts have their striking 'candles' of white or pink spring blossom, while Laburnum has been widely cultivated for its decorative hanging sprays of yellow flowers. Look at the colour, shape and size of the flowers – but also look closely to observe details such as whether the petals are double or single and the length of the flower stalks. Make a note, too, of how the flower grows on the tree. For example, are they growing singly or in clusters? This detailed approach is particularly useful when trying to identify one specific tree within a family of similar trees.

Using fruit for identification

A tree's fruit can often provide an instant source of identification. The Beech tree's three-sided nuts (known as mast), housed in a spiky husk, are instantly recognisable, as are the English Oak's acorn and the London Plane tree's ball of hairy seeds. Cones, the seed-bearing structures of a conifer tree, are very useful in distinguishing among different conifers. The flat-based, rounded, brown cone of a Stone Pine, for example, is different from the rounded, globular cone of a Swamp Cypress. As with flowers, it is important to observe how the fruit is carried on the tree. For example, is it on a stem or does it sit directly on the branch?

Using buds for identification

Identifying deciduous trees in winter, when their leaves have fallen, is particularly challenging. However, in these cases, a tree's winter buds can often offer a valuable clue. Make a note of the way the buds are arranged on the tree: whether they are opposite or alternate. Look at the shape, colour and texture. A Horse Chestnut has a large, sticky bud while the Ash has a smooth, black bud.

Using the shape of the tree for identification

Certain trees have distinctive shapes that make them very easy to identify. The Traveller's Palm, for example, has long, green leaves, which form a distinctive fan shape, marking it out clearly from other palms. Columnar trees – that is those that grow straight upwards – include the Cypress and the Lombardy Poplar. The shapes of deciduous trees and the patterns of their branches can be a great help in identifying them in winter when they are without their leaves. The English Oak, for example, has a very recognisable spreading shape with its thick, twisting branches, which marks it out from other deciduous trees. Bear in mind, of course, that the height and shape of a tree does depend upon its habitat, with excessive competition or crowding from other trees affecting its growth.

THE ANATOMY OF A TREE

BARK AND TRUNK

The tree's bark resembles armour or a protective skin, offering a waterproof protective layer against disease, water loss, insects, animals and even, in some cases, against forest fires. Bark allows the tree to breath, being perforated with minute breathing pores known as lenticels, which allow oxygen to pass into the tree. Lenticels can become blocked with pollution and certain trees shed and renew their bark; the London Plane is such a tree and is renowned for its ability to grow in a polluted environment, hence its popularity as an urban street tree.

The structure of tree bark:

Underneath the outer bark is a layer of inner bark, known as the phloem. This carries out an important function, transporting large quantities of nutrients throughout the tree and carrying the sugars made by the leaves to the rest of the tree. As the phloem dies it becomes absorbed into the outer bark. Beneath the phloem is a thin layer of generative stem cell tissue called the cambium. The word 'bark' is, in general, used to describe everything that lies outside the cambium. The cambium is the growing layer which widens the tree, producing both phloem cells on the outside and what is called xylem on the inside. In trees growing where there are distinct seasons, the pattern of producing new xylem creates visually distinguishable 'growth rings', allowing these trees to be dated. In good growing years these rings are wider than in bad growing years, so the growth rings also offer information on the climate that the tree was experiencing. The xylem on the inside of a tree carries water and nutrients from the roots up to the leaves. As the xylem cells die they harden, losing the ability to carry water, becoming what is known as the heartwood, while the living xylem on the outside forms the sapwood. Xylem cells are made up of cellulose, a glucose-based carbohydrate, and lignin, a complex organic polymer that gives wood its structural strength. Many tree barks also have a second layer of cambium, outside the primary cambium layer, specifically producing cork cells. Cork aids the tree by preventing water loss, repelling pests and also by being relatively fireproof. The Cork Oak in the Mediterranean and Africa's Baobab trees both have thick layers of cork, a light, waterproof substance, which is harvested and used for various purposes, most famously to cork wine bottles.

*Above: The gnarled shape and silvery leaves of the olive tree (*Olea europaea*) are a characteristic sight of the Mediterranean region although it is also grown in other parts of the world, including South America, Australia and South Africa.*

LEAVES

The leaves of trees vary hugely in shape and size, from the short, narrow needles produced by conifers to the Traveller's Palm's immense, broad 3m (10ft) long leaves. Trees are often categorised as being either broad-leaved or narrow-leaved. Another popular division based on their leaves is into deciduous trees, which shed all their leaves in the autumn when they enter a dormant state then grow fresh leaves the following spring, and evergreen trees, which loose some of their leaves throughout the year but always have some on the tree. Evergreens have tough leathery leaves that can cope in extreme climate conditions, including drought and bitter cold. Despite their diverse appearance, however, leaves always perform the same function.

Put simply, leaves are the tree's food factory. They are the site of photosynthesis, the process whereby sugars are made from water and carbon dioxide, using the energy from sunlight. Because of their dependence on sunlight, leaves are characteristically positioned to enjoy maximum light absorption.

Photosynthesis takes place in the presence of a green pigment known as chlorophyll, found within tiny cell-like vessels called chloroplasts inside the leaf. Oxygen is the waste product of photosynthesis, released into the atmosphere.

The structure of a tree leaf

A leaf is covered on its upper and lower surfaces by a layer of cells known as the epidermis. In turn, the epidermis is coated on the outside by a protective, waxy covering known as the cuticle, which prevents water loss. Little breathing holes, called stomata, transfer carbon dioxide and oxygen into and from the leaf. Water is also lost through the stomata, a process known as transpiration. In the leaves of broad-leafed trees a network of visible veins carries the xylem, bearing the raw materials for photosynthesis such as water and minerals from the roots, and the phloem, carrying the sugars made by the leaves to the other parts of the tree. Evergreen needles carry out the same function, but in a more compact form.

When it comes to describing leaf shapes, botanists have developed a whole specialised vocabulary of terms to ensure accuracy and aid correct identification. Broadly speaking, however, leaves can be divided into three groups:

- Simple leaves come in a wide variety of shapes, from round to oval, and can have smooth edges, serrated edges or be 'lobed' (that is, indented).
- Compound leaves, at first glance, look like separate leaves growing off the same stalk. In fact, however, the whole stalk and its leaflets all grow from the same leaf bud, making it one leaf.
- Needles, as their name suggests, are narrow, elongated leaves, found on all conifers.

Autumn leaf colour

In temperate countries, the changing colours of the leaves on deciduous trees are one of the signs, and indeed beauties, of the autumn season, a signal that winter is approaching. As trees prepare for the winter, a change in season signalled by the shorter days, they begin to close down their functions, ready to live off the food collected and stored from the summer months. The green chlorophyll in their

*Opposite: The Swamp Cypress (*Taxodium distichum*) has strikingly colourful foliage, which is fresh green in spring and turns gold to red in the autumn, so it is often planted for ornamental purposes.*

*Above: The cones of the Maritime or Cluster Pine (*Pinus pinaster*), which are long and slender and grow in small clusters.*

leaves, which mediates photosynthesis, disappears from the leaves, revealing the yellow and orange pigments. The bright reds and purples that are particularly spectacular are created by glucose trapped in the leaves after photosynthesis stops. The Maple tree, with its gorgeous red autumn colour, is a classic example of this. Leaves that turn brown, like those of the Oak, are coloured by the waste products left in the leaves.

TREE REPRODUCTION

A tree's primary functions are to grow and to reproduce. Central to tree reproduction are cones and flowers. Cones are the reproductive systems of conifer trees (whose name comes from the Latin for 'cone-bearing') and are gymnosperms, or seed plants whose seed is not fully enclosed within an ovary. Angiosperms technically means plants whose seeds are completely enclosed within an ovary, but is also used simply to mean flowering plants, with flowers being the angiosperm's reproductive system. In the plant kingdom, angiosperms are far more prevalent than gymnosperms; there are around 50 times more species of flowering trees than of coniferous trees.

Coniferous trees bear male or female cones, but never hermaphrodite (combining both sexes) cones, while flowers are often hermaphrodite, combining both male and female parts. The majority of conifers bear both male and female cones on the same individual tree and they are known as monoecious. In some species, such as the Yew or the Holly, trees are either male or female and they are known as dioecious.

Tree flowers vary enormously in appearance, from tiny, unobtrusive flowers to large, striking blossoms, such as the magnolia. Despite the visual diversity, the basic structure of most tree flowers is similar, consisting of a stamen (the male reproductive organ producing pollen), the stigma (which receives the pollen), the style (linking the stigma to the ovary) and the ovary (containing ovules that, once fertilised, become seeds).

Pollination

Both coniferous and flowering trees use their cones and flowers to produce pollen for fertilisation. As trees are static, they rely on wind, insects, birds and animals to spread their pollen and cause vital fertilisation. As the wind is indiscriminate, trees that rely on the wind for pollen dispersal tend to have smaller, more modest flowers than those trees that are seeking to attract insects, birds or animals. Insects play a vital role in tree reproduction, with the best known insect pollinators being bees, butterflies and moths – although flies and beetles are also important. Over 60 per cent of tree species in equatorial regions are pollinated by insects. Scented flowers, rich in nectar, are one device that the tree uses to attract potential pollinators. Trees pollinated by insects tend to produce large-grained, sticky pollen that will stick to the insects. In a strategy to ensure efficient insect pollination, the Horse Chestnut tree changes the colour of a flower once it has been pollinated to one that deters bees, to encourage them to visit other flowers.

Birds, such as humming birds, also act as tree pollinators, attracted by brightly coloured flowers. Certain trees also rely on bats for pollination, producing strongly scented, rather than fragrant, night-opening flowers to attract them. Wind pollination is common in the colder, northern temperate regions of the world, where insects are less common. All conifers rely on wind pollination, producing generous amounts of pollen in order to disperse it as widely as possible. Broad-leafed trees that also rely on wind pollination include Birch trees, with their distinctive, drooping catkins, laden with pollen. Once the process of fertilisation has been completed, the tree then has the challenge of dispersing its seed as widely as possible.

Seed dispersal

Trees have adopted many different strategies to spread their seeds. Conifers that rely on the wind for pollination also use the wind to disperse their small seeds, opening up the cones that contain the seeds in response to heat and humidity levels. These small, light seeds often come with little papery wings that allow them to be blown away as far as possible from the parent tree. Certain trees that use wind dispersal have developed impressively aerodynamic winged seeds, known as keys, to maximise the distance they can travel. The Ash and Sycamore are notable examples of trees with keys; both are very effective at spreading themselves.

Certain trees wrap their seeds inside an appetising fruit, so that animals will take away and eat the fruit but spit out the seeds, or so that both fruit and seeds will be eaten and passed through the animal's digestive system. Brightly coloured berries and fruit, such as scarlet Holly berries, attract the attention of birds. Tree fruits range in size from small berries, such as Rowan or Elder berries, to much larger fruit, such as the tropical durian or papaya.

Some trees enclose their seeds within tough outer casings and these seeds we think of as nuts. Nuts, such as the macadamia, often have extremely hard shells. Famously, the Brazil nut, with its notoriously tough shell, can be opened by the powerful-jawed agouti, a cat-sized rodent – and for the tree it has the useful habit of burying a cache of Brazil nuts for future consumption. Squirrels, of course, are noted for burying stores of nuts, which then germinate and grow.

There are a few trees that have ingenious ways to ensure prime conditions for their seeds' survival. Among them is the Coastal Redwood – its cones will not release their seeds until first heated in forest fire. This somewhat high-risk strategy ensures that the seeds emerge into an environment free of other competing plants.

Water is a great carrier of seeds. The Alder tree, which often grows by water, takes advantage of this, as its seeds are able to float on water and so can be carried away. Coconut palms, growing by the sea, have sent their large coconuts on long journeys by dropping them into the ocean waves. The sensually shaped coco-de-mer, the seeds of a palm tree growing on the Seychelles, occasionally find their way across the Indian Ocean, washing up on Indian beaches where their origins were a source of mystery for many centuries. The seeds of the Jaury Palm, which grows in the Amazon rainforest, are eaten and transported by fish when the forest floods.

Germination

Tree seeds contain a plant embryo, together with a food store. Once a seed finds a suitable location, and if the conditions are right, it will germinate at once. It does so by first sending out a root, which instinctively grows downwards. The root provides the embryo inside the seed with additional food and moisture, to allow the tree to develop. The seed also often contains chemically coded instructions on when to germinate – including delaying devices to ensure germination does not take place until the conditions are favourable.

Self-propagation

Certain trees are able to reproduce through suckering, a process in which surface roots send up sprouts that eventually grow into new trees. Willows and Aspens are particularly noted for this ability.

Below: The brightly coloured berries of the Holly (Ilex aquifolium) attract birds, which spit out the seeds, so spreading them over a wider area.

CONIFERS

AND MAIDENHAIR

MAIDENHAIR
(GINKGO)
GINKGO BILOBA

This graceful tree is the sole surviving species of a group of seed trees that existed over 200 million years ago and it is often thought of as a 'living fossil'. Its distinctive fan-shaped leaves, which turn bright yellow in the autumn, resemble those of the maidenhair fern, hence its popular name. Revered by Chinese and Japanese Buddhist monks and seen as a symbol of longevity, hope and unity, the ginkgo was widely planted in Buddhist temple gardens where many magnificent, ancient specimens can be found to this day. Ginkgo nuts are a delicacy in China and Japan and its fine-grained wood is used for carving. Today, although thought to be extinct in the wild, its attractive appearance and ability to withstand pollution means it exists as a cultivated tree, planted in parks, gardens and yards around the world.

Height: Up to 30m (100ft)
Type: Deciduous
Bark: Grey-brown
Leaf: Fan-shaped green leaf
Flower: Trees either male or female. Male catkins yellow, 2–4cm ($^{7}/_{8}$–1$^{1}/_{2}$in), in bunches. Female flowers green 4mm ($^{1}/_{2}$in) knobs paired on 4cm (1$^{1}/_{2}$in) stalks
Fruit: greenish yellow plum-like fruit with a fleshy coating and edible kernel

COMMON LARCH
(EUROPEAN LARCH)
LARIX DECIDUA

Indigenous to the central hilly regions of Europe, the long-lived larch is now widely planted in Europe and North America. The reason for this is its strong, rot-resistant timber, and there is also the advantage that the larch is a fast-growing tree, making it a popular choice for plantation forestry. Its durable timber has been particularly used for railway sleepers, tunnel supports in mines and staircases. It is also a traditional source for Venice or larch turpentine, obtained by tapping full-grown trees. It is unusual for a conifer in that it is deciduous, a fact indicated by its Latin name *decidua*. Bright green in the spring and golden in the autumn, the larch is also popular for ornamental reasons and so is often planted in parks and gardens.

HEIGHT: 40m (130ft)
TYPE: Deciduous
BARK: Grey and smooth when young, fissured when old
LEAF: Flat, soft needles, growing in whorls on side shoots and singly on main shoots
FLOWER: Male: yellow; Female: pink-red
FRUIT: Oval cones, brown with straight scales and visible bracts

CEDAR OF LEBANON
CEDRUS LIBANI

This majestic, slow-growing, long-living tree has long been a symbol of immortality and strength. It is mentioned many times in the Bible, and its wood is thought to have been used to build King Solomon's temple. Its natural habitat is found in Syria, the Taurus Mountains in Turkey, and Mount Lebanon. As its name suggests, it is closely associated with Lebanon – so much so, that its distinctive outline appears on the Lebanese flag. In fact for the first 40 years of its life it grows in a conical shape, before developing its distinctive level foliage plates. During the eighteenth century it became the fashionable tree to plant in the gardens and estates of stately homes and today is a popular ornamental tree for parks.

HEIGHT: Up to 40m (130ft)
TYPE: Evergreen
BARK: Red-brown bark with shallow fissures
LEAF: Grey-blue to dark green needles, growing in whorls on side shoots and singly on main shoots
FLOWER: Male: yellow-brown when open, up to 6cm (2¼in) long; Female: bright green with purple tinge, 7–15cm (2¾–6in)
FRUIT: Erect, barrel-shaped cones, grey-green, ripening to purplish-brown

PICEA ABIES NORWAY SPRUCE

This slender, conical spruce, widely grown throughout northern Europe, is best known as Europe's Christmas tree. The custom of having a decorated Christmas tree inside the home was brought over from Germany and popularised in Britain by Prince Albert, Queen Victoria's husband. The Norway spruce, with its symmetrical shape, dark green foliage and distinctive pine fragrance, continues to be a traditional festive feature of many European households at Christmas. The steady-growing spruce is also Europe's most important timber tree, valued for its straight, strong timber. Cultivated in plantations, it has many commercial uses, among them the manufacture of paper pulp and packing cases and for general carpentry. It is also one of the main woods traditionally used by violinmakers, chosen for its lightness, flexibility and strength.

HEIGHT: Up to 50m (165ft)

TYPE: Coniferous

BARK: Coppery pink when young, turning purple-grey and cracked

LEAF: Short, dark green needles

FLOWER: Separate, upright clusters. Male: red; Female: dark red

FRUIT: Pendent, slender, cylindrical, light brown cones, up to 20cm (8in) long, with jagged scales

STONE PINE (UMBRELLA PINE)
PINUS PINEA

HEIGHT: 20m (66ft)
TYPE: Evergreen
BARK: Grey-brown with deep fissures
LEAF: Long, dark green needles, growing in pairs
FLOWER: Separate clusters at the end of stalks. Male: golden; Female: green
FRUIT: Very broad, flat-based, rounded, cones up to 10cm (4in) across, ripening from green to glossy brown, containing large, edible seeds

A classic sight throughout the Mediterranean region, the stone pine has a distinctive, wide-spreading, domed crown on top of a slender trunk creating a parasol-like effect, which explains its other name, 'umbrella pine'. Cultivated in Europe for almost 2,000 years, the stone pine is often planted along walkways or avenues because of its attractive appearance and shade-providing properties. It is also greatly valued for its edible seeds, known as pine nuts. These small, protein-rich, ivory-coloured kernels, with their sweet, mild flavour and oily texture, are used in Mediterranean cookery, most famously as a key ingredient of pesto, a sauce for fresh pasta. As pine nuts are very difficult to harvest they are a costly ingredient.

(CLUSTER PINE) MARITIME PINE
PINUS PINASTER

Native to the Mediterranean region, the maritime pine is found from Portugal to Morocco. Tolerant of salt spray and able to grow in sandy conditions, this tree thrives along the coast; consequently it is often planted to form a shelterbelt along exposed coasts in order to stabilise sandy soil. A striking example of its ability to reclaim land is the forest of Landes in Gascony, France, covering 1 million hectares (2,471,100 acres), which was created on the site of a huge swamp that was drained during the nineteenth century and planted with maritime pines. Historically, the tree was cultivated for its resin, from which turpentine was derived. Today, however, it is used for timber and is an important forestry tree in France, Portugal and Spain.

HEIGHT: Up to 40m (130ft)
TYPE: Evergreen
BARK: Red-brown, fissured
LEAF: Very long, green needles growing in pairs
FLOWER: Male: yellow, at base of shoots; Female: red, in clusters at ends of shoots
FRUIT: Slender, shining brown cones, in small clusters

PINUS LONGAEVA BRISTLECONE PINE

Found only in the White Mountains of Eastern California, South Nevada and Central Utah, the slow-growing Bristlecone pine is famed as one of the world's longest living trees. The oldest specimen, the precise location of which is kept secret, is a tree known as 'Methuselah', thought to be nearly 5,000 years old. The discovery of these ancient trees is credited to a scientist called Dr Schulman, working in the 1950s. Prior to this, it had been assumed that the oldest trees were the world's biggest, the giant sequoias. Despite the bristlecone's incredible longevity, the actual appearance of the tree is gnarled and stunted rather than imposing. Growing as it does in an extremely harsh mountain environment, with conditions ranging from cold, snowy winters to parched, hot summers, the bristlecone grows extremely slowly, hence its impressive long lifespan.

HEIGHT: 15m (50ft)
TYPE: Evergreen
BARK: Reddish brown with deep fissures
LEAF: Short green needles in fives
FLOWER: Male: purple-red; Female: purple
FRUIT: Red-brown, drooping cones, with slender spines that soon break off

PINUS SYLVESTRIS SCOTS PINE

Britain's only native pine tree is also the most widely spread of all European conifers, found growing in Scandinavia and also in southern Spain. A pioneer species, which can thrive in poor soil, it is a long-lived tree capable of reaching 250–300 years in age. Despite being a tall tree it has a narrow trunk, which in mature trees can be just over 2.5m (8ft) wide. It is a keystone species in Scotland, providing a home for many plants, insects, birds and animals, such as the rare red squirrel. Its naturally resin-rich timber is resistant to decay and widely used in building. Traditionally, its tall, straight, flexible trunks were valued for masts and spars, while the Vikings used its leaves as a valuable source of Vitamin C, drinking pine beers to ward off scurvy.

HEIGHT: Up to 36m (120ft)
TYPE: Evergreen
BARK Orange-red to grey-brown, layered into plates and cracked and fissured when mature
LEAF: Long, blue-grey needles growing in pairs
FLOWER: Male: yellow, in clusters at base of shoots; Female: crimson, in pairs at ends of shoots
FRUIT: Slim, egg-shaped cones, up to 7cm (2¾in) long, green ripening to brown

BHUTAN PINE
(BLUE PINE)

PINUS WALLICHIANA

This tall, graceful conifer is native to the Himalayas, and is found growing from Afghanistan to Nepal and Bhutan, from where it derives its name. Preferring to grow on mountain slopes, the Bhutan pine can thrive quite happily at altitudes above 3,800m (12,470ft). When young it forms a conical shape, but as it matures its crown broadens. It is a resilient tree, notably resistant to air pollution. In forestry it is often planted to protect steep slopes.

HEIGHT: Up to 50m (165ft)
TYPE: Evergreen
BARK: Orange-grey with tiny fissures
LEAF: Drooping green needles, growing in fives
FLOWER: Male: yellow, in clusters; Female: green-yellow, in groups of up to six
FRUIT: Long cones, green maturing to brown

DOUGLAS FIR
PSEUDOTSUGA MENZIESII

Native to North America, this majestic, fast-growing tree is highly valued for the fine quality of its timber, so consequently it is grown commercially throughout North America, Europe, Australia and New Zealand. Its fine-grained, durable timber is widely used in construction work, from houses, bridges and boats to telegraph poles and flagstaffs. An impressively tall tree, frequently reaching heights over 75m (250ft), its trunk is often free of branching for the first 33m (110ft). Its hanging, egg-shaped cones grow with distinctive three-pointed bracts from each scale. The tree was first introduced to Britain in 1827 by the plant-hunter David Douglas, in whose honour it is named.

HEIGHT: Up to 100m (325ft)
TYPE: Evergreen
BARK: Grey-brown, corky, fissured
LEAF: Green needles with white banding underneath
FLOWER: Male: yellow, beneath shoots; Female: red, on shoots
FRUIT: Pendent cone, brown, 3-pronged bracts

KAURI
AGATHIS AUSTRALIS

Native to New Zealand and only found there, the long-lived, majestic kauri tree was revered by the indigenous Maori people. While the young tree grows in conical form, as the tree matures it sheds its lower branches, resulting in a straight, clean trunk topped by a broad canopy. It is truly an impressive tree, capable of reaching over 50m (165ft) in height and with a massive trunk. The tallest surviving kauri, found in the Waipoua Forest in Northland, is called *Tane Mahuta* or Lord of the forest and stands 51.2m (168ft) tall with a trunk 5.5m (18ft) in diameter. Once New Zealand was widely forested with kauri trees. During the nineteenth century, however, European settlers felled the trees in enormous numbers for their valuable timber. Today the kauri forest covers only 7,285 hectares (18,000 acres), a fraction of its original size.

HEIGHT: Up to 50m (165ft)
TYPE: Evergreen
BARK: Smooth grey, shedding thick flakes
LEAF: Leathery oblong leaves
FLOWER: Male: cylindrical; Female: spherical, grey
FRUIT: Cones

MONKEY PUZZLE
(CHILE PINE)
ARAUCARIA ARAUCANA

The distinctive and striking monkey puzzle tree is native to Chile, where it was declared a national monument in 1990 by the Chilean Ministry of Agriculture. Its large, flavourful and nutritious seeds are a traditional staple food of the Pehuenche Indians, a Chilean mountain tribe. Its introduction to Europe in 1795 came about when Royal Navy surgeon and plant-collector Archibald Menzies, dining with the Viceroy of Chile, noticed an unusual type of nut on the table and slipped five into his pocket, sprouting them on the voyage home. This exotic-looking tree became very fashionable and was widely planted in European botanical gardens and parks during the nineteenth century. Indeed, today it is thought that there are more monkey puzzle trees in Europe than in its native Chile, where it is endangered.

HEIGHT: 30–40m (100–130ft)
TYPE: Evergreen
BARK: Smooth, grey-brown, marked by rings
LEAF: Leathery, triangular, sharp-tipped, green leaves
FLOWER: Male: erect, yellow-brown cones with whorled scales; Female: globe-like, green cones
FRUIT: Spherical brown cone with overlapping, spiny bracts

PACIFIC YEW
TAXUS BREVIFOLIA

HEIGHT: Up to 20m (66ft)
TYPE: Evergreen
BARK: Scaly brown
LEAF: Flat, dark green
needles growing spirally
on the stem
FLOWER: Male: pale
yellow; Female: tiny,
green globes
FRUIT: Oval seed in fleshy
red coating

Native to the Pacific Northwest of North America, this small evergreen tree, unassuming in appearance, possesses striking medicinal properties. During the 1990s it was discovered that the tree contained a toxin called taxol, which could be used in chemotherapy to treat breast, lung and ovarian cancer. The taxol is contained in largest quantities in the bark of the Californian yew, which led to mass bark-stripping of the tree, which was already rare. As a direct result of this over-exploitation the Californian yew has become an endangered species in the wild, though it is now being grown on plantations in an attempt to satisfy the demands of the pharmaceutical industry.

(COMMON YEW, ENGLISH YEW) YEW
TAXUS BACCATA

Found throughout Europe, the yew tree also grows as far east as northern Iran and as far south as North Africa's Atlas Mountains. A slow-growing evergreen, it is one of the world's long-lived trees capable of living for thousands of years. Britain's oldest tree, found in Fortingall in Scotland, is a yew tree, estimated to be 3,000–5,000 years old. All parts of the tree are extremely poisonous, so it must always be treated with respect. Yew wood, however, has long been valued for its extreme hardness and resistance to water. The wood's elasticity and ability to withstand great tension made it the classic wood for the long bow. There is much folklore associated with the yew tree, which was often seen as a symbol of eternal life, and it is frequently found planted in Christian churchyards.

HEIGHT: Up to 25m (82ft)

TYPE: Evergreen

BARK: Grey-brown with scaly patches revealing purple-red bark underneath

LEAF: Flat, sharp-pointed green needles, growing in a spiral around upright shoots

FLOWER: Male and female nearly always on separate trees. Male: spherical catkins, beneath shoots; Female: tiny buds, near shoot-ends

FRUIT: Single seed encased in fleshy, red coating

ITALIAN CYPRESS
CUPRESSUS SEMPERVIRENS

Native to the Mediterranean region, the elegant, slender, dark green cypress tree forms a classic element of the landscape in countries such as France and Italy. Its narrow columnar shape and dense foliage covering most of the tree give it a striking appearance and it is widely grown as an ornamental tree, often planted in lines along drives and walkways. It is also a tree that has long associations with mourning.

HEIGHT: Up to 30m (100ft)
TYPE: Evergreen
BARK: Grey-brown, ridged
LEAF: Tiny, scale-like, dark green leaves in sprays
FLOWER: Male: yellow-brown; Female: green
FRUIT: Dull grey-brown cones, up to 3cm (1¼in) long, each scale with a blunt knob

LEYLAND CYPRESS (LEYLANDII)
X CUPRESSOCYPARIS LEYLANDII

HEIGHT: Up to 40m (130ft)
TYPE: Evergreen
BARK: Reddish grey with ridges
LEAF: Green, scale-like, in sprays
FLOWER: Clusters at tips of shoots. Male: yellow; Female: green
FRUIT: Spherical brown cones

Created in Britain during the late nineteenth century, this vigorous hybrid, widely planted as a fast-growing hedging plant, has become the subject of much controversy in recent years. It originated on the Leighton Park estate, Powys, as a cross between a Nootka Cypress and a Monterey Cypress and was subsequently grown from cuttings. Unless carefully pruned the Leyland cypress can grow rapidly out of hand and so has been the cause of many disputes between neighbours. Its dense foliage, however, makes it a popular nesting choice for birds, which appreciate the good cover it provides.

(EASTERN) RED CEDAR
JUNIPERUS VIRGINIANA

Native to North America, this evergreen tree is misleadingly named, being in fact a juniper tree rather than a cedar. It has long been valued for its fragrant, soft, pinkish red wood, which is resistant to rot and is avoided by moths so has traditionally been used for wardrobes and clothes chests. Its fine-grained timber was also the premier wood for pencils. A pioneer invader tree, it is often found on wasteland. It is also widely planted as a windbreak and to protect soil from erosion. Its evergreen foliage provides good roosting and nesting for birds, while its fruits are eaten by both birds, such as the cedar waxwing, and animals, such as raccoons and foxes.

HEIGHT: Up to 18m (60ft)
TYPE: Evergreen
BARK: Reddish brown
LEAF: Green needle-like juvenile leaves, scale-like adult leaves
FLOWER: Male and female on separate trees. Male: yellow; Female: green
FRUIT: Blue-grey berries

JUNIPER
JUNIPERUS COMMUNIS

This slow-growing evergreen, often growing
as a shrub rather than as a small tree,
naturally occupies a large geographic range
since it is found in Canada, the northern
USA, Europe, North Africa and Japan. It has
long been valued for its aromatic, dark blue
berries, used medicinally by the Ancient
Egyptians and the Romans. Traditionally,
juniper berries were also used to end
unwanted pregnancies. Although juniper
berries are used in cooking, for example in
game stews, their best-known use these days
is as an essential flavouring for gin. In fact,
the name gin derives from the French word
ginevre, meaning juniper. Fragrant juniper
wood is also traditionally used for smoking
and preserving meats. It is a popular dwarf
conifer for rock gardens as well, with many
cultivars now available.

HEIGHT: Up to 6m (20ft)
TYPE: Evergreen
BARK: Grey-brown
LEAF: Short, prickly blue-green needles growing in
whorls of three
FLOWER: Male and female on separate trees, Male:
yellow; Female: green
FRUIT: Spherical, fleshy berries, taking three years to
ripen from green to black

GIANT SEQUOIA
(WELLINGTONIA)
SEQUOIADENDRON GIGANTICEUM

The giant sequoia lives up to its name, with one specimen, nicknamed 'General Sherman', believed to be the world's largest tree. Standing an imposing 82.6m (271ft) tall, General Sherman has a diameter of 8.2m (27ft), is estimated to weigh around 2,000 metric tonnes (4,410,000lb) and thought to be 2,100 years old. The giant sequoia is found only in California, growing in what has been designated the Sequoia National Park where the groves of soaring trees make an awe-inspiring sight. Its thick bark, which can be up to 61cm (24in) thick, is so spongy that it can be 'punched' without causing injury. Despite the tree's majestic appearance its timber is, in fact, very soft.

HEIGHT: Up to 90m (300ft)
TYPE: Evergreen
BARK: Dark red, thick and spongy
LEAF: Small, pointed, scale-like
FLOWER: Male: pale-green, rounded, at tips of shoots;
   Female: green, oval, at stem tips
FRUIT: Barrel-shaped, pendent cone, 5–8cm
   (2–3¼in) long

(CALIFORNIAN REDWOOD) COAST REDWOOD
SEQUOIA SEMPERVIRENS

The world's tallest living tree, nicknamed the 'Stratosphere Giant', is a majestic coast redwood growing in California, which in 2004 measured 112.8m (370ft). Its precise location remains secret in order to protect the tree. A slow-growing tree, the coast redwood is capable of reaching not only great height but also great age, being able to live for over 2,000 years. The thick, tannin-rich bark protects the coastal redwoods from insects and also makes them resistant to forest fire. Coastal redwood timber, however, was valued for its lightness and beauty and intensive logging during the nineteenth century saw the destruction of many old-growth redwoods. Today these long-lived giants of the natural world are found only on a narrow strip of land in America, restricted to 72 groves on the western slopes of the Sierra Nevada, California.

HEIGHT: Over 110m (360ft)
TYPE: Evergreen
BARK: Reddish brown, spongy, deeply fissured
LEAF: Dark green, sharp-pointed needles
FLOWER: Separate clusters on same tree. Male: yellow-brown, rounded; Female: red-brown, bud-like
FRUIT: Diamond-shaped brown cone

DAWN REDWOOD
METASEQUOIA GLYPTOSTROBOIDES

This striking deciduous conifer, today found growing naturally only in China, is often called a 'living fossil'. It was only discovered by chance by a forester in 1941, in the countryside in Szechuan province, China. Upon further investigation the unfamiliar tree that the forester had found turned out to belong the genus *Metasequoia*, which hitherto had only been known in fossil form and was thought to have been extinct for 5 million years. Both its remarkable history and ornamental appearance have resulted in its being planted in botanical gardens around the world, but it remains critically endangered in the wild.

HEIGHT: Up to 45m (148ft)
TYPE: Deciduous
BARK: Dark red, spongy
LEAF: Dark green, soft, flat needles
FLOWER: Male: yellow in pairs on stalks; Female: green, rounded, in hanging clusters
FRUIT: Pendent, rounded cones, dark brown when mature

(BALD CYPRESS) SWAMP CYPRESS
TAXODIUM DISTICHUM

Native to the south-eastern USA, the swamp cypress is noted for its ability to thrive in waterlogged or flooded conditions with its roots submerged for several months. In order to cope with these conditions the tree has developed distinctive, spongy, mound-shaped, aerial roots known as 'knees' or 'penumatophores', which grow around the trunk. It is also thought that these 'knees' may help support the tree in these marshy conditions. Typically conical, this tall deciduous conifer has strikingly colourful foliage, which is fresh green in spring and turns gold to red in the autumn, and so it is planted for ornamental purposes in parks and gardens.

HEIGHT: Up to 50m (165ft)
TYPE: Deciduous
BARK: Pale orange-grey
LEAF: Short, narrow leaves
FLOWER: Male: yellow hanging catkins; Female: green, in small clusters
FRUIT: Rounded cone with small spines, ripening in one year

FLOWERING
TREES

PRIMITIVE ANGIOSPERMS

NUTMEG
MYRISTICA FRAGRANS

Indigenous to the Molucca islands in Indonesia, the nutmeg tree is the source of two spices: nutmeg and mace. The nutmeg is the kernel of the tree's seed while mace is the dried lacy 'aril' or sheath that surrounds the nut. These spices were introduced to the West by Arab traders and were well known throughout Europe by the twelfth century. In 1514 the Portuguese took over the Molucca islands, establishing a monopoly on the lucrative nutmeg trade, which they maintained for nearly 100 years. The Dutch succeeded in ousting them and in turn retained a monopoly on the trade for over 150 years. Eventually the nutmeg was grown in French and British colonies, such as Mauritius and Penang. Today nutmeg trees are widely cultivated on the Caribbean island of Grenada.

HEIGHT: Up to 18m (60ft)
TYPE: Evergreen
BARK: Grey-brown
LEAF: Shiny, dark green, alternate, oval, pointed
FLOWER: Male and female flowers usually found on different trees, pale yellow, waxy, bell-shaped
FRUIT: Yellow, fleshy, smooth drupe with ridge, splitting open when ripe to reveal brown, oval seed, covered in web of red mace

DRIMYS WINTERI WINTER'S BARK

Native to Chile and Argentina, this flowering tree is named after seaman Captain William Winter, who came across the tree while sailing through the Straits of Magellan as part of Sir Francis Drake's fleet during the sixteenth century. Captain Winter used the aromatic bark to treat his ship's crew as a protection against scurvy and introduced it to England. In South America winter's bark is used to treat toothache and also stomach disorders. Botanically the tree belongs to a family of evergreen shrubs and small trees that have acrid or aromatic bark, hence the generic name from the Greek *drimus*, meaning acrid.

HEIGHT: Up to 15m (50ft)
TYPE: Evergreen
BARK: Smooth, reddish brown
LEAF: Oval, green, alternate, leathery
FLOWER: Clusters of up to 10; 5–7 white or cream petals, red sepals
FRUIT: Small, round, green seed pod, ripening to black, in clusters, containing black seeds

TULIP TREE
LIRIODENDRON TULIPIFERA

Native to the eastern states of North America, where it is one of the region's tallest trees, this striking tree is related to the magnolia family. Its popular name derives from its large tulip-shaped flowers, which are yellow-green in colour with orange corollas. With its distinctive summer flowers and bright green foliage that turns yellow-gold in the autumn, the tulip tree is a particularly attractive tree. It was introduced to Britain in 1688, where it was planted for ornamental purposes in parks and gardens. In its native North America its fine-grained, soft timber, known as whitewood, is used for plywood and pulp.

HEIGHT: Over 30m (100ft)
TYPE: Deciduous
BARK: Pale grey-green with white furrows
LEAF: Deeply lobed
FLOWER: Six petals, pale green at the edge and deep orange at the centre
FRUIT: Cone-like, woody unseeded fruit with one wing

SOURSOP ANNONA MURICATA

HEIGHT: 7.5–9m (25–30ft)
TYPE: Evergreen
BARK: Red-brown
LEAF: Dark green, smooth, oval, pointed
FLOWER: Three greenish-yellow outer petals, three pale yellow inner petals, fragrant
FRUIT: Green-yellow, distorted oval fruit, 10–30cm (4–12in) long, with spines, black glossy seeds

This tropical fruit tree, native to northern South America and the West Indies, is now cultivated in many parts of the world including South East Asia, India and Polynesia. It is a low-branching, bushy tree, valued for its distinctive, large fruit which can grow anywhere on its trunk or branches. The soursop fruit grows in a characteristic, lop-sided ovoid shape and has a green, leathery skin covered with soft spines. Its flesh inside is bright white, soft and juicy with a distinctive yet subtle fresh flavour. Soursop drinks are popular in Caribbean and Latin American countries. The tree also has many uses in traditional herbal medicine; for example, its leaves are thought to have sedative properties, while the juice of the fruit is used as a diuretic.

CINNAMOMUM CAMPHORA CAMPHOR LAUREL

Native to China and Japan, this large evergreen has many uses. In its native countries it is grown commercially for its medicinal oil and the white crystalline compound known as 'camphor', obtained by distilling its bark, leaves and roots. Camphor, with its penetrating odour and numbing effect, has many traditional medicinal uses, ranging from treating toothache to alleviating back pain. It is also used in the manufacture of moth repellents, celluloid and explosives. A fast-growing, dense-crowned tree, it has been planted for its shade and as a windbreak. In Australia, where it was introduced as an ornamental park tree, it is now considered an invasive species.

HEIGHT: Up to 30m (100ft)
TYPE: Evergreen
BARK: Grey-brown, fissured
LEAF: Glossy, leathery, oval, alternate, with a distinctive camphor scent when crushed
FLOWER: Tiny, greenish yellow, in small panicles
FRUIT: Small, round, black berries, less than 1cm ($^3/_8$in) long

CINNAMON
CINNAMOMUM VERUM
(CINNAMOMUM ZEYLANICUM)

Famous for its fragrant bark (often confused with cassia bark), the cinnamon tree is native to Sri Lanka (known formerly as Ceylon), from where the finest quality cinnamon comes, but it is also cultivated in the Seychelles, Southern India and Malaysia. The dried inner bark of the cinnamon tree is sold in curled strips known as 'quills', or in powdered form, and is widely used as a spice in many cuisines around the world. Highly valued during the fifteenth and sixteenth centuries, it proved a very lucrative crop to the Portuguese who discovered it growing wild on Ceylon in 1505. They subsequently took over the island, followed in turn by the Dutch and then the British. In addition to its culinary attributes, cinnamon is valued as an insect repellent and for its anti-microbial properties.

HEIGHT: Up to 18m (60ft)
TYPE: Evergreen
BARK: Pale, pinkish brown
LEAF: Oval, opposite, waxy, green
FLOWER: Tiny, off-white or pale yellow in clusters
FRUIT: Oval drupe, dark purple to black, less than 1cm (³/₈in) across

(PERFUME TREE) YLANG YLANG
CANANGA ODORATA

Despite its unassuming appearance, this evergreen tree is highly valued for the fragrant essential oil produced from its flowers. A fast-growing species native to the Philippines and Indonesia, it is now widely cultivated throughout tropical Asia, the Pacific Islands and India. Its richly perfumed flowers are striking in appearance, resembling long-armed starfish and ranging in colour from pale green to yellow. The oil is obtained by distilling the flowers, with 900–1,500kg (1,984–3,307lb) of flowers required to produce 18–30kg (40–88lb) of essential oil. The oil, which is traditionally credited with aphrodisiac qualities, is widely used in perfumery and also in aromatherapy to treat high blood pressure.

HEIGHT: Up to 25m (82ft)
TYPE: Evergreen
BARK: Pale grey
LEAF: Green, oval to elliptic, may be slightly wavy along the edges
FLOWER: Clusters, green becoming yellow, six, long, twisted, hanging petals, fragrant
FRUIT: Small, oval, black berries, in clusters

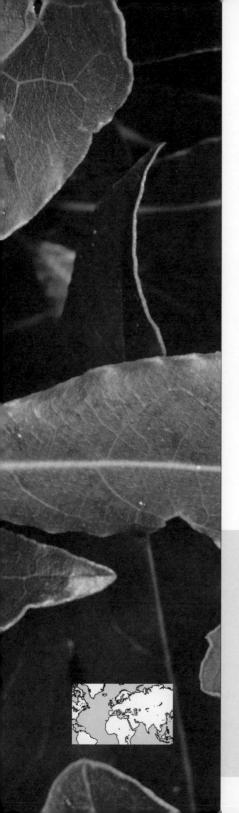

BAY TREE
(SWEET BAY, POET'S LAUREL)
LAURUS NOBILIS

Indigenous to the Mediterranean region, the bay tree has a venerable and noble reputation. It was sacred to the god Apollo in Greek and Roman mythology and was the 'laurel' woven into wreaths used to crown victorious athletes, warriors and poets in classical times. Today it is best known as a culinary herb, with its aromatic leaves one of the most widely used herbs in European and North American cooking, adding flavour to dishes from pasta sauces to stews. Its shiny, evergreen leaves and the fact that it can be clipped into topiary shapes means that it is also valued as an ornamental plant, classically found in formal gardens grown in pots in a neat lollypop shape.

HEIGHT: Up to 18m (60ft)
TYPE: Evergreen
BARK: Dark grey, smooth
LEAF: Shiny, dark green, oval with pointed tip, aromatic when crushed
FLOWER: Male and female on separate trees, in clusters. Small, yellow with six petals, male with numerous stamens
FRUIT: Purple to black rounded, fleshy berries 1cm ($^3/_8$in) across, on female plants

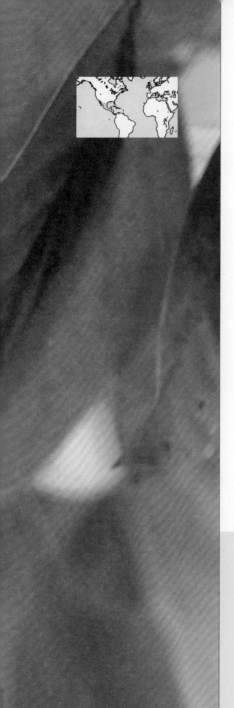

AVOCADO
(AVOCADO PEAR OR ALLIGATOR PEAR)
PERSEA AMERICANA

Native to Central America, the avocado tree has been cultivated in that region for over 7,000 years. It was prized then, as now, for its green-skinned, pear-shaped fruit, which has smooth, subtle-flavoured, buttery-textured flesh. Of all fruits the avocado has the highest protein and oil content, making it an important source of energy. Today it is grown commercially in many parts of the world, including California and Florida in the United States, Israel, Australia and the Canaries. Such is the fruit's popularity that there are over 500 varieties, with Hass being a well-known cultivar. Guacamole, a well-known dish made from avocados, is thought to be a modern-day version of the Aztec ahuaca-mulli or avocado sauce.

HEIGHT: Up to 18m (60ft)
TYPE: Evergreen
BARK: Dark grey-brown
LEAF: Dark green, glossy, elliptical
FLOWER: Racemes, pale green to yellow-green, three petal-like lobes, with nine stamens, fragrant
FRUIT: Green to black drupe, about 10–15cm (4–6in) long, with large, round to oval seed

SASSAFRAS ALBIDUM SASSAFRAS

Native to eastern North America, this tree has historically had many varied uses. Sassafras 'tea' was made by steeping its roots and it was also formerly a key flavouring in root beer. Its essential oil has been used to add fragrance to perfumes and soaps and is also known as a mosquito repellent. In Cajun and Creole cookery, dried, powdered sassafras leaves, known as 'filé', are used to thicken and flavour gumbo, a spicy stew.

HEIGHT: Up to 25m (82ft)
TYPE: Deciduous
BARK: Grey-brown
LEAF: Unlobed, two-lobed or three-lobed
FLOWER: Male and female on separate trees, green-yellow, petalless, borne in dropping, few-flowered racemes
FRUIT: Dark blue, egg-shaped, single-seeded drupe with thick red stalk

MONOCOTYLEDONS

SCREW-PINE
PANDANUS TECTORIUS

This distinctive looking tree grows from north-eastern Australia throughout the islands of the tropical Pacific ocean to Hawaii. A coastal dune plant, it is able to thrive in loose soil through its aerial 'prop roots', which grow from the main trunk and act as additional, stabilising anchors. Throughout the Pacific islands the screw-pine has been widely used in a variety of ways. Its leaves were woven or plaited into mats, baskets, thatch and sails, while its large edible fruit, which resembles a pineapple, was historically a major food source for the islanders, eaten raw or cooked.

HEIGHT: Up to 9m (30ft)
TYPE: Evergreen
BARK: Prickly
LEAF: Long and narrow with serrated edges
FLOWER: Male and female on separate trees. Male: in clusters 30cm (12in) long, of tiny fragrant flowers surrounded by white or cream bracts; female: in flowerheads
FRUIT: Resembles a pineapple, consists of several woody segments

QUIVER TREE
ALOE DICHOTOMA

Indigenous to the arid areas of southern Africa, the redoubtable, slow-growing quiver tree, with its thick trunk and rounded crown, is a distinctive sight. Its characteristic forked branches are reflected in the species name *dichotoma*, from dichotomous meaning 'forked'. Its common name derives from the fact that the light branches were traditionally hollowed out and used as quivers by the San tribe. Its sharp-edged trunk and leaves make it a favoured tree for weaver birds to construct communal nests in because it offers protection from snakes and jackals. Its bright yellow, nectar-filled flowers also attract sugar birds.

HEIGHT: Up to 9m (30ft)
TYPE: Evergreen
BARK: Sharp-edged, golden-brown scales
LEAF: Sharp-toothed, narrow, pointed blue-green leaves in rosettes
FLOWER: Tiny, yellow on branched spikes 30cm (12in) high
FRUIT: Smooth, shiny capsule

GRASS-TREE XANTHORRHEA AUSTRALIS

HEIGHT: Up to 2m (6ft)
TYPE: Evergreen
BARK: Thick, corky bark
LEAF: Long, thin green
FLOWER: Small, white or cream, clustered together on tall spikes
FRUIT: Capsule, with hard, black seeds

Unique to Australia, this extraordinary-looking tree is today an icon of the Australian bush. A tough, slow-growing evergreen, the grass-tree can live for up to 600 years. It has tall, striking spikes of densely packed white flowers, which grow up from the leaves. Historically, this plant was a key staple for the Aboriginal people. The light, straight flower stalks were used as the butt ends for spears, while resin flakes, gathered from the base of the tree, were melted and used as a glue to fix spear shafts and tips and also to waterproof canoes. The young tender stalks of the leaf bases were eaten, its flower stalks soaked to make a sweet drink and its seeds ground into flour. Today its distinctive appearance has made the grass-tree a valued plant in Australian landscape gardening.

DRACAENA CINNABARI DRAGON TREE

This distinctive, primitive plant, sometimes nicknamed the 'inside-out umbrella tree', is unique to the island of Soqotra. This isolated island in the Indian Ocean, off the Horn of Africa, is home to around 850 plant species – over a third of which are only found on Soqotra. Legend has it that the dragon tree sprang up from the blood shed by a dragon and an elephant as they battled to the death. In ancient times the tree was prized as the source of highly valued cinnabar, the crimson-red resin produced from its leaves and bark. Cinnabar was used as a pigment for paint, to treat burns and to stain glass, marble and the wood for Italian violins. Today, cinnabar is still used by the dwellers on Soqotra for dyeing, decorating, to treat stomach problems and as lipstick.

HEIGHT: Up to 15m (50ft)
TYPE: Evergreen
BARK: Rough-textured, silvery grey
LEAF: Broad-based spiky leaves in clusters
FLOWER: Pale yellow, in clusters
FRUIT: Berry, yellow ripening to black

JOSHUA TREE
YUCCA BREVIFOLIA

Found in the harsh environment of the Mojave Desert in south-western California, Nevada, Utah and Arizona, this rugged dessert plant is the largest yucca in the world. Legend has it that its name was given to it by Mormon pioneers because of its resemblance to the biblical figure of Joshua, exhorting them with outstretched arms to continue westward. The native Americans wove its tough leaves into baskets and ate its flowers and seeds, while European settlers used its timber for fencing. It is pollinated by the yucca moth, which – attracted by the tree's pungent-smelling flowers – lays her eggs in them; the hatched larvae then survive by eating yucca seeds.

HEIGHT: Up to 12m (40ft)
TYPE: Evergreen
BARK: Grey-brown, ridged
LEAF: Sharp-edged, spiky, leathery, strap-shaped
FLOWER: Bell-shaped, cream, yellow or green, in upright clusters at ends of branches
FRUIT: Fleshy capsule, pale to red-brown

BETEL
ARECA CATECHU

HEIGHT: Up to 20m (66ft)
BARK: Green, ringed
TYPE: Evergreen
LEAF: Glossy, deep green, pinnate with many narrow leaflets
FLOWER: Male and female on the same plant in branched inflorescences. Tiny, creamy-white, fragrant; male: close to tip; female: at base
FRUIT: Oval, 5cm (2in) in diameter, yellow to orange to red

Thought to have originated in South East Asia, the betel palm is widely cultivated throughout the Asian tropics, notably in India. The reason for this mass cultivation is the ancient custom of chewing betel nuts, the seeds of the betel palm. In India – the largest consumer of betel nuts – the most basic betel chew or 'paan' consists of pieces of betel nut eaten with lime and betel pepper leaves, resulting in a distinctive red staining of the mouth and saliva. The effect of chewing betel is stimulating and energising. In Ayurvedic medicine, too, the betel nut has many uses. Today, however, long-term betel chewing is regarded as carcinogenic.

(TODDY PALM) PALMYRA PALM
BORASSUS FLABELLIFER

Native to India and South East Asia, this tree is widely cultivated in many tropical countries and has many uses. In India its leaves are used for thatching and also for making mats, baskets, writing material and fans. Its hard, heavy timber is also valued. This particular palm is also tapped for its sugary syrup, known as 'toddy', which can be fermented to make palm wine. The toddy is also boiled down and concentrated to make palm sugar or jaggery. In addition, the Palmyra palm has many uses in traditional medicine, with different parts of the tree used to treat conditions ranging from coughs to heartburn.

HEIGHT: Up to 21m (70ft)
TYPE: Evergreen
BARK: Grey-brown
LEAF: Fan-shaped, stiff, green
FLOWER: Male and female separate, bunches at base of leaves
FRUIT: Rounded, black when ripe, containing hard-shelled seeds

COCONUT PALM
COCOS NUCIFERA

There are so many uses for the coconut palm that it has been called 'the tree of life'. In South Asia the coconut is a symbol of selfless service, prosperity and generosity. Its origins are uncertain, with both Melanesia and tropical America posited. Today, the coconut palm is widely cultivated throughout the tropics where it provides food and drink, timber and thatching (from its leaves). It flourishes on seashores, with palm-fringed beaches being a classic tropical image. The 'meat' of the coconut is eaten in its own right and also used to produce coconut milk, copra (dried coconut meat) and coconut oil. Its sugary sap is fermented to make an alcoholic drink or concentrated to form palm sugar. The outer husk of the coconut is used to make coir fibre, traditionally used for fishing nets. In Ayurvedic medicine, too, the coconut is widely used.

HEIGHT: Up to 30m (100ft)
TYPE: Evergreen
BARK: Grey, marked by leaf scars
LEAF: Pinnate, with strap-shaped leaflets, green
FLOWER: Shoots at leaf axils; yellow-orange, lance-shaped petals; male: at tips; female: at base
FRUIT: Large drupe, with a tough, smooth outer husk, ripening from green to grey, a fibrous middle layer and a hard inner layer

OIL PALM

ELAEIS GUINEENSIS

Native to West Africa, the oil palm is today also widely cultivated in South East Asia for its oil, with this tree offering the highest yield of all tropical oil-producing plants. Palm oil, traditionally used in West Africa for domestic cooking, is today widely used in food processing, appearing in foods from margarines to cakes. The oil is contained in the plum-sized fruit and obtained both from the flesh and the kernel. Since its introduction into Indonesia and Malaysia, large tracts of indigenous rainforest have been cut down to make way for large-scale plantations, a cause of concern to environmentalists. Today South East Asia is the world's largest producer of palm oil – and plans to use palm oil in bio-diesel suggest that the market for this oil may well increase.

HEIGHT: Up to 20m (66ft)
TYPE: Evergreen
BARK: Grey, ringed with leaf scars
LEAF: Green, pinnate with slender leaflets in pairs
FLOWER: Inflorescences, 10–30cm (4–12in) long
FRUIT: Bunches of plum-like drupes, black when ripe

KITUL PALM (JAGGERY PALM OR FISHTAIL PALM)
CARYOTA URENS

HEIGHT: Up to 30m (100ft)
TYPE: Evergreen
BARK: Grey, marked with leaf scars
LEAF: Long, bipinnate with fishtail-shaped leaflets
FLOWER: Inflorescences, up to 6m (20ft) long, cream-coloured
FRUIT: Red drupe, 2cm ($^7/_8$in) wide, containing one or two seeds

Grown mainly in India and Sri Lanka, the kitul palm plays a key part in these countries' rural economies. One of its prime uses is as a source of sweet sap used to make jaggery or palm sugar. In Sri Lanka there is a special caste, known as *hakuru*, who make their living from kitual-tapping and jaggery-making. A single tree can be tapped for sap for 10–15 years, after which it is generally harvested for its timber. The sap is also fermented to make an alcoholic drink, as with the toddy palm. The sheathing of the leaf bases is uses to make kitul fibre, which resembles horsehair. The seeds, however, contain oxalic acid and can be toxic. Today it is being planted for ornamental purposes as well as practical ones.

SAGO PALM
METROXLYON SAGU

The sago palm is widely cultivated throughout the tropics. It is grown for the edible starch, known as sago, contained within its trunk, which was historically an important staple food. To extract sago, the tree is first allowed to reach maturity (around 12–15 years of age), then chopped down just before it flowers, when it has built up a reserve of starch in its trunk. The trunk is split and the pith scraped out, then washed and strained to obtain the pure starch. The dried starch is sago meal, widely used in animal feed, while granulated starch is known as 'pearl' sago.

HEIGHT: Up to 15m (50ft)
TYPE: Evergreen
BARK: Brown, marked by leaf bases
LEAF: Green, pinnate, feathery
FLOWER: Branched inflorescences, 3m (10ft) tall
FRUIT: Straw-coloured drupe

DATE PALM
PHOENIX DACTYLIFERA

The date palm has been cultivated for its sweet, edible fruit for thousands of years. Grown in many countries around the world today, the date palm's place of origin is uncertain but archaeological evidence shows that the date palm was known in Ancient Egypt and Mesopotamia. The date is a staple food in the desert regions of the Middle East and North Africa and is regarded as a symbol of fertility. In Muslim countries, dates are one of the foods traditionally eaten when the sun sets during the fasting time of Ramadan. These sweet fruit are often eaten simply as they are, but can also be filled with nuts or used in baking.

HEIGHT: Up to 30m (100ft)
TYPE: Evergreen
BARK: Grey-brown, covered with leaf bases
LEAF: Blue-green, long, pinnate with narrow leaflets
FLOWER: Male and female on separate trees. Small, whitish, in axillary, pendent clusters up to 1.2m (4ft) long
FRUIT: Clusters of oblong drupes, each up to 4cm (1½in) long, dark orange when ripe, containing one seed

TRAVELLER'S PALM
RAVENALA MADAGASCARIENSIS

This attractive tree, native to Madagascar, is not a true palm, being more closely related to the banana. Its decorative appearance comes from the 'fan' of broad leaves, which grows across the tree giving it a striking and distinctive outline. This attractive foliage has made it a popular ornamental choice for planting in parks, gardens and palace and temple grounds in the tropics. Its popular name is derived from the fact that thirsty travellers could find water contained in the hollow leaf bases. Traditionally, the tree's leaves are used for thatching and it is also tapped for its sugary sap.

HEIGHT: Up to 12m (40ft)
TYPE: Evergreen
BARK: Green with leaf rings
LEAF: Broad, paddle-shaped, green leaves, shredded by the wind
FLOWER: Small, white, borne in clusters, held in large green bracts
FRUIT: Brown berry, containing black seeds in blue aril

DICOTYLEDONS

MACADAMIA MACADAMIA INTEGRIFOLIA

HEIGHT: Up to 21m (70ft)
TYPE: Evergreen
BARK: Rough, brown
LEAF: Glossy, dark green, in whorls of three
FLOWER: Tiny, white, cream or pale pink, borne in dangling tassels
FRUIT: Spherical nut, hard green outer layer

Native to Australia, the macadamia tree is cultivated both there and in Hawaii, where the tree was introduced around 1882. The nut was only 'discovered' in the second half of the nineteenth century, and named by a botanist after his friend Dr John Macadam, but is today one of Australia's best-known food plants. It is grown commercially for its distinctive, mellow-flavoured nuts, which grow in clusters, each nut housed in a hard, poisonous husk and shell. The nuts take around 7 months to mature, whereupon they fall to the ground from where they are harvested. Today, Hawaii accounts for around 90% of world production of macadamia nuts. The nuts have a high oil content of 75–80% and this edible oil is sometimes extracted, but primarily the nuts are sold whole.

BUXUS SEMPERVIRENS BOX

This slow-growing evergreen, native to chalk and limestone habitats, has a long history of use by mankind. Fine-grained dense boxwood is the hardest of any European tree, notable for not warping and for the fact it can be cut into the finest pattern without breaking. Historically, boxwood was used to make measuring instruments, including rulers, printing blocks, engraving plates and pulley blocks. The tree's dense, evergreen foliage, combined with its slow rate of growth and ability to withstand clipping, has made it a popular plant for hedges and topiary – something that continues to be true today. All parts of the box tree, particularly its leaves and seeds, are poisonous, yet it is also a plant that has long been used medicinally, traditionally to treat fevers, smallpox and the bites from 'mad dogs'.

HEIGHT: Up to 6m (20ft)
TYPE: Evergreen
BARK: Fawn, smooth then finely fissured
LEAF: Glossy, ovate to oblong leaves, often with a notched tip
FLOWER: Clusters of 5–6 stalkless males surrounding one short-stalked female: pale yellow, petalless; fragrant
FRUIT: Capsule with three split horns, becoming brown and papery, releasing black seeds

LONDON PLANE
PLATANUS X HISPANICA

Thought to be a hybrid between the Oriental plane (*Platanus orientalis*) and the American plane or Buttonwood (*Platanus occidentalis*), which manifested itself in southern Europe in the mid seventeenth century, this hardy tree is now closely associated with the city of London where it is widely planted in streets, squares and parks. It is a remarkably tolerant tree, putting up with pollution, drought and compacted soil, hence its popularity for urban planting. Its distinctive flaking bark enables the tree to renew its bark when clogged with pollutants. When not pruned, the London plane can be a magnificent, round-crowned tree, and there are some fine London specimens which were planted over 200 years ago. Its Latin name derives from the Greek *platanos*, referring to the tree's broad leaves.

HEIGHT: Up to 45m (148ft)
TYPE: Deciduous
BARK: Grey with distinctive patchy flaking, revealing buff coloured bark beneath
LEAF: Green with variable lobbing
FLOWER: Male and female in separate, petalless clusters on same tree; male: yellow; female: reddish
FRUIT: Pendent, spiky globes, covered with bristles, green ripening to brown

RED RIVER GUM
(MURRAY RED GUM OR RED GUM)

EUCALYPTUS CAMALDULENSIS

Native to Australia, the Red River gum grows throughout most of mainland Australia, where it is one of the continent's most widespread tree species. It is also a plantation species in many parts of the world, being one of the most widely planted eucalyptus species. It grows beside watercourses and on flood plains, preferring deep, moist clay soil, and plays an important part in stabilising riverbanks. Commercially, its timber is used in the construction industry for railway sleepers, fencing, flooring, veneer and marquetry, firewood and charcoal production. As an important producer of quality pollen and nectar, it is a valuable source of honey.

HEIGHT: 20–45m (66–148ft)
TYPE: Evergreen
BARK: Mottled, white, brown or red bark
LEAF: Alternate, grey-green, oval to lanceolate
FLOWER: Axillary clusters of 7–11, creamy white flowers
FRUIT: Semi-spherical capsule, yellow seeds

BLUE GUM (TASMANIAN BLUE GUM)
EUCALYPTUS GLOBULUS

HEIGHT: 15–45m
(50–148ft)
TYPE: Evergreen
BARK: Smooth, creamy
white, peeling in red
flakes
LEAF: Alternate, very long,
lanceolate to sickle-
shaped, dark green
FLOWER: 5cm (2in) wide,
with numerous
stamens, white
FRUIT: Ridged, greyish,
woody capsule

Native to the Australian island of Tasmania and found also
on the Australian mainland in southern Victoria and New
South Wales, this tall, fast-growing tree is Tasmania's floral
emblem. The juvenile leaves are covered with a blue-grey,
waxy bloom, hence its common name 'blue gum'. It is an
important timber species, producing pale, hard, durable
timber. It is grown commercially for oil, fuel, telegraph
and mine poles, construction timber and pulpwood for
paper. It is also planted to dry out swampy land,
particularly in central Africa, Italy and Turkey. So effective
was the tree in draining marshy land, home to malaria-
carrying mosquitoes, that its fragrant leaves were thought
to have anti-malarial properties. The aromatic oil from the
tree, high in anti-bacterial properties, is used to treat
influenza, colds and sinusitis and, in liniments, for bruises,
sprains and wounds.

CLOVE
SYZYGIUM AROMATICUM

Native to the Moluccas, in East Indonesia, the clove tree is today cultivated widely throughout the tropics, particularly in Zanzibar, the Malagasy Republic and Indonesia. It is grown for its immature flower buds, known as cloves, which are harvested and dried for use in cooking, medicine, perfumery and the tobacco trade (with *kretek* being the clove-scented cigarettes favoured by the Indonesians). Cloves were used in Ancient China in the third century BC and in India for many centuries. Such was clove's commercial value as a spice that first the Portuguese in 1514, then the Dutch in the early seventeenth century took control of the Moluccas, using draconian measures in order to enjoy a profitable monopoly. The tree also produces clove oil, extracted from its leaves and unripe fruit, which is used in dentistry.

HEIGHT: 15m (50ft)
TYPE: Evergreen
BARK: Smooth, pale brown bark
LEAF: Glossy, elliptical, dark green leaves
FLOWER: Bell-shaped, in threes on a short panicle, pale pink, yellow or green, fragrant
FRUIT: Oblong, 2.5cm (1in) long, red or purple when ripe

GUAVA
PSIDIUM GUAJAVA

Thought to be native to Central America and the West Indies, this fruit tree is now grown widely in tropical and subtropical regions. Archaeological remains in Peru show that human beings were eating guavas as long ago as 800 BC. The Spanish and Portuguese introduced the fruit from Central America to other countries and it has been well-established in India and South East Asia since the seventeenth century. Its strongly-scented fruits, high in vitamin C, are the reason for the tree's popularity, with numerous cultivars now grown commercially. Throughout the regions in which it is grown guavas are eaten raw or cooked in pies, cakes, puddings, custards, ices and also made into a thick paste known as 'guava cheese'. Guava juice is a popular fruit beverage as well.

HEIGHT: 10m (33ft)
TYPE: Evergreen
BARK: Pale reddish brown, flaking off in large pieces to reveal grey-green inner bark
LEAF: Opposite, ovate to oblong, green
FLOWER: 2.5cm (1in) wide with numerous white stamens, white
FRUIT: Round, lumpy fruit, up to 10cm (4in) long, yellowish-green or pinkish

POPULUS TREMULA ASPEN

This fast-growing, deep-rooted tree is found widely throughout Europe, North Africa and western Asia. It is best-known for its fluttering leaves, sensitive to the lightest breeze, hence its Latin name *tremula*, which means 'trembling'. These moving leaves produce a distinctive noise, rather than like rain falling. In British folklore, the aspen was the tree used for the Cross on which Christ was crucified, since when the unfortunate tree has trembled in guilt and sorrow. Traditionally, its light, soft wood was used for clogs and arrows. The charcoal made from aspen wood was particularly valued for gunpowder. Today, it is often used for lightwood packing cases.

HEIGHT: Up to 30m (100ft)

TYPE: Deciduous

BARK: Pale grey, pitted with small, black diamonds

LEAF: Shiny, green, round, toothed

FLOWER: Male and female green catkins up to 5cm (2in) on separate tree. Male: with red anthers

FRUIT: Small, green catkin-like capsules, seeds with white, fluffy hairs

WHITE WILLOW

SALIX ALBA

Found throughout Europe and western Asia, the willow grows best in damp soil and is frequently found growing on riverbanks or on land next to ponds. The willow tree has long been valued for its medicinal properties. In the fifth century BC the Greek physician Hippocrates used a bitter powder extracted from the bark of the willow tree to treat aches and pains and to reduce fevers. During the nineteenth century it was discovered that willow bark was a natural source of salicin, which could be isolated in its crystal form and was to be the precursor of the modern aspirin.

HEIGHT: Up to 25m (82ft)
TYPE: Deciduous
BARK: Grey-brown, fissured
LEAF: Lanceolate leaves, covered with silky white hairs giving the leaves a grey-white appearance
FLOWER: Male and female catkins on separate trees. Male: 5cm (2in) long with yellow anthers; female: green
FRUIT: Green capsule with white-haired seeds

PARA RUBBER HEVEA BRASILIENSIS

HEIGHT: Up to 30m (100ft)
TYPE: Semi-deciduous
BARK: Grey-brown
LEAF: Alternate, trifoliate with elliptic leaflets
FLOWER: Greenish white, petalless, borne in axillary panicles
FRUIT: Three-sectioned capsule, greenish brown

Native to the Amazon Basin, this tropical tree was for long time the source of the world's rubber supply. The rubber is obtained from latex, a white, sap-like extract within the rubber tree's trunk that is released by tapping. Initially, rubber trees simply grew wild but as demand grew for rubber they were cultivated in plantations. For a long time, Brazil was the only country where rubber trees could be cultivated and rubber exports, accordingly, were a mainstay of the Brazilian economy. The development of vulcanization in 1839, which stabilised rubber, added to its uses and economic value. By 1898 a rubber plantation had been successfully established in Malaysia, marking the end of Brazilian dominance of the rubber trade. Today, although rubber is still cultivated in the tropics, synthetic rubber is widely used.

PROSOPIS GLANDULOSA (HONEY MESQUITE) MESQUITE

Native to the Southern United States and Mexico, this small, hardy tree grows in sandy flatlands and deserts. It is a drought-resistant tree, able to survive in arid conditions with the aid of its extremely long tap-root, which helps it reach water. Its seed pods were traditionally an important food source for Native American tribes in North America, who ground both seeds and pods into a nutritious meal for making bread, and also used them for making tea and syrup. The tree also has medicinal uses, particularly the gum that exudes from its trunk, which is used as an eyewash, to treat wounds and burns and for diarrhoea. Its dense, slow-burning, smokeless timber is used for fencing and as an aromatic charcoal for barbecues. Mesquite is also known for its characteristic smoky-flavoured honey, produced by the bees that feed on its flowers.

HEIGHT: Up to 15m (50ft)
TYPE: Deciduous
BARK: Reddish brown, fissured
LEAF: Alternate, bipinnate with 6–17 linear to oblong green leaflets
FLOWER: Axillary spikes, small, greenish yellow
FRUIT: Long flat pods, 10–30cm (4–12in) long, with oblong seeds

FEVER TREE

ACACIA XANTHOPHLOEA

Native to Africa, the graceful fever tree grows in low-lying swampy ground, often by lakes or rivers. Its generic name *Acacia* comes from the Greek *acanthi*, meaning 'spine', while its specific name derives from the Greek *xanthos*, meaning' yellow', and *phloios*, meaning 'bark'. The name 'fever tree' is due to European settlers' mistaken belief that the tree, which is found growing in marshy ground, caused malaria. It is a popular nesting tree for birds as its thorns deter predators, such as snakes. Traditionally, its hard, heavy timber is used for fencing. Its attractive shape, feathery foliage and golden yellow blossoms (in addition to the fact that it is easy to propagate) have made it a popular tree for landscape gardening.

HEIGHT: 15–25m (50–82ft)
TYPE: Semi-deciduous
BARK: Greenish yellow, coated in yellow powder
LEAF: Alternate, bipinnate, green
FLOWER: Golden yellow, ball-like, borne in clusters
FRUIT: Yellow-brown to brown pod

JUDAS TREE
CERCIS SILIQUASTRUM

Native to southern Europe and western
Asia, the low-growing Judas tree, in
Christian folklore, was reputed to be the
tree from which Judas Iscariot hanged
himself. In spring the tree takes on an eye-
catching and picturesque appearance,
coming into bloom with clusters of pink
flowers growing from branches and from
the trunk itself. The flowers are edible,
eaten in salads or coated in batter and fried
as fritters or pickled as a substitute for
capers. The hard, fine-grained wood is
traditionally used for veneer work. The
tree's ornamental nature has made it a
popular choice for parks and gardens.

HEIGHT: Up to 10m (33ft)
TYPE: Deciduous
BARK: Dark grey-brown with small rugged ridges when
  mature
LEAF: Kidney-shaped, untoothed, grey-green, smooth
FLOWER: Sweet pea-like, magenta-pink
FRUIT: Flat brown pods

LABURNUM

LABURNUM ANAGYROIDES

Native to the mountainous regions of central Europe, the laburnum is also known as the 'golden rain' or 'golden chain' tree, both references to its abundant, hanging sprays of bright yellow blossom, which flower in the spring. Its ornamental appearance has made it a popular garden tree, despite the fact that it is actually very poisonous – especially its seeds, contained in narrow, pea-like pods. Its dark brown, hard wood was used as a substitute for ebony, but today it is cultivated primarily for its graceful looks.

HEIGHT: Up to 9m (30ft)
TYPE: Deciduous
BARK: Greenish brown
LEAF: Green, alternate with three elliptic leaflets
FRUIT: Pea-like, golden yellow, in drooping racemes up to 30cm (12in) long
FRUIT: Hairy, brown pod

TAMARIND TAMARINDUS INDICA

HEIGHT: Up to 25m (82ft)
TYPE: Evergreen
BARK: Grey-brown, rough, fissured
LEAF: Alternate, pinnate with 10–20 pairs of oblong, green leaflets
FLOWER: Racemes at sides and ends of shoots, up to 2.5cm (1in) long, cream to yellow with red markings
FRUIT: 18cm (7in) long, rough-skinned, brown pod

Originally from Africa, the tamarind tree has grown in India since prehistoric times and grows widely throughout the world's tropical and subtropical regions. It is grown commercially as a food tree for its tamarind pods, which contain a sticky, brown, tart pulp, with India being the world's only producer of tamarind on a commercial scale. Tamarind pulp is widely used fresh or in concentrate form as an acidifying agent in Indian and South East Asian cookery, adding a characteristic sourness to dishes such as curries and relishes. It is also eaten fresh and used to make sweets and drinks. In traditional Indian medicine it is used to treat diabetes, fevers and intestinal infections. Its pods are harvested at different stages of ripeness according to how they will be used.

ERIOBOTRYA JAPONICA (JAPANESE MEDLAR) LOQUAT

Thought to originate in China where it has been cultivated for over 1,000 years, this evergreen fruit tree is now naturalised and cultivated around the world, including California, South America, Japan, India, the Mediterranean and Australia. The tree is grown primarily for its delicate-flavoured, apricot-coloured fruit, which grow in clusters, and today Japan is the world's largest producer. At one time the loquat was particularly prized as the first soft fruit to mature, ripening in spring, ahead of peaches and apricots. The fruit can be eaten fresh, as it is, or in fruit salads, or stewed and is also made into jam and jelly.

HEIGHT: Up to 6m (20ft)
TYPE: Evergreen
BARK: Dark grey, flaking
LEAF: Alternate, whorled at branch tips, lanceolate, dark green, glossy, toothed
FLOWER: Terminal racemes, large, white, fragrant
FRUIT: Oval to pear-shaped pome, orange when ripe, with large seeds

HAWTHORN
(MAY, QUICKTHORN, WHITETHORN)
CRATAEGUS MONOGYNA

Native to Europe, the hardy hawthorn, with its thorny branches, has long been used to grow hedges to keep in animals and to divide land. The name hawthorn, in fact, comes from the Anglo-Saxon *hagathorn* with *haga* meaning 'hedge'. When growing naturally as a tree, rather than as a planted hedge, the hawthorn thrives in open ground, developing a distinctly gnarled trunk when old. Its old country name 'May' is thought to derive from the fact that it flowers profusely in that month. It is a tree wreathed in folklore and beliefs. Thought by the Romans to ward off sickness, sprigs of hawthorn were attached to newborn babies' cradles. In Christian folklore, the hawthorn was thought to be the tree from which Christ's crown of thorns was made and so, as the plant that touched Christ, it offered protection from evil.

HEIGHT: Up to 10m (33ft)
TYPE: Deciduous
BARK: Brown with shallow ridges
LEAF: Deeply lobed, glossy, green leaves
FLOWER: Borne in dense clusters on shoots, creamy white,
FRUIT: Oval red pome, 1.5cm (½in) wide

QUINCE

CYDONIA OBLONGA

Cultivated quince trees are descended from the small, wild quince tree that originated in the Caucasus. The tree has long been cultivated in the Middle East and the Mediterranean for its distinctive fruit. Resembling a lumpy pear, the quince has an exquisite fragrance but, with the exception of a few cultivars, has to be cooked before eating, which causes it to take on a pinkish colour. In Greek mythology the quince was sacred to Aphrodite, the goddess of love, and it is thought to be the fruit described as the 'golden apple' of the Hesperides. In Spain quince paste, known as *membrillo*, is traditionally eaten with cheese, while in Iranian cuisine the quince is used in meat stews.

HEIGHT: Up to 8m (26ft)

TYPE: Deciduous

BARK: Grey and smooth when young, flaking off in irregular plates when mature

LEAF: Dark green, long, alternate, ovate to oblong, untoothed

FLOWER: Terminal, solitary, large with five white to pink petals

FRUIT: Large, fragrant, pear-shaped pome, up to 10cm (4in) long, downy, yellow when ripe

CRAB APPLE
MALUS SYLVESTRIS

Native to Europe, the crab apple grows in hedgerows and at the edges of woodlands. It is one of the ancestors of the modern cultivated apple and is used as graft stock by commercial apple growers. Its small, yellow fruit, known as crabapples or crabs, are extremely sour. In medieval European cooking, crabapples were traditionally used to make an acidic condiment known as 'verjuice'; this added a sour flavour to dishes in the way that a squeeze of lemon juice does in modern cookery. Today, however, crabapples, which are high in pectin, are primarily used to make crabapple jelly. The tree's hard, heavy, close-grained wood has been used to make items such as clubs and wedges.

HEIGHT: 8–12m (26–40ft)
TYPE: Deciduous
BARK: Pale brown to grey when young, grey-brown when mature, peeling in flakes
LEAF: Alternate, elliptic to obovate, toothed, dark green, glossy
FLOWER: Borne in clusters on short shoots, white, tinged with pink
FRUIT: Spherical, green to yellowish-red pome, up to 4cm (1½in) across

CULTIVATED APPLE MALUS DOMESTICA

HEIGHT: Up to 15m (50ft)
TYPE: Deciduous
BARK: Shallowly scaly, grey to brown
LEAF: Alternate, ovate with serrated margins, green
FLOWER: Pink buds, opening into large, white flowers, tinged with pink
FRUIT: Spherical, brown, green, yellowish red pome, at least 4cm (1½in) wide

The apple tree is now widely cultivated in temperate regions around the world. Today there are hundreds of apple cultivars, all grown for their fruit, which ranges in flavour, according to variety, from sour cooking apples to sweet-fleshed dessert apples. A standard fruit in western Europe for several centuries, the apple is famously shown in depictions of the temptation of Eve, even though the Bible does not specify what type of tree bore the fruit of the knowledge of good and evil. As well as being eaten raw, apples are cooked in dishes such as pies and cakes.

PRUNUS ARMENIACA APRICOT

The apricot tree originated in northern China, where it was cultivated before 2000 BC. Today the tree is widely grown in the warmer, temperate regions of the world, prized for its sweet, edible, orange-fleshed, soft fruit. Turkey is the world's largest producer of apricots. Although ripe apricots can be eaten raw, it is also a popular dried fruit, with dried apricots from Hunza in Pakistan particularly valued for their depth of flavour. In the Middle East, sheets of dried apricot paste (which is then diluted to make a drink), are popular, especially during the fasting month of Ramadan. Apricot jam is another traditional way of preserving the fruit.

HEIGHT: Up to 10m (33ft)
TYPE: Deciduous
BARK: Red-brown, smooth and glossy
LEAF: Alternate, ovate to rounded with tapered tip, finely toothed, glossy green
FLOWER: Large with five, white to pink petals
FRUIT: Ovoid, fleshy drupe, orange-red when ripe with large, single seed

GEAN (WILD SWEET CHERRY, MAZZARD)

PRUNUS AVIUM

The gean or wild sweet cherry is the parental species of the cultivated sweet cherries. Its small, dark red fruits are either sweet or bitter, but never sour. Its specific name *avium* comes from the Latin *avis*, meaning 'bird', thought to be a reference to the fact that birds love cherries as much as humans. As an easy-to-establish, fast-growing tree, the gean is also a popular timber species. Cherry tree wood, with its attractive appearance, is used for furniture-making, and particularly for veneer. Traditionally. it was also a favourite wood from which to make pipes.

HEIGHT: Up to 25m (82ft)
TYPE: Deciduous
BARK: Glossy, red or purple-brown, peeling in horizontal bands
LEAF: Alternate, elliptic to oblong, toothed, dull green
FLOWER: Borne in clusters, ivory-white,
FRUIT: Spherical drupes, red when ripe

PLUM
PRUNUS DOMESTICA

HEIGHT: Up to 10m (33ft)
TYPE: Deciduous
BARK: Grey to purple-brown, widely fissured
LEAF: Alternate, elliptic to obovate, wrinkled, toothed, green
FLOWER: Clusters on short stalks, white
FRUIT: Ovoid drupe, yellow, red or purple with large single seed

The origins of the cultivated plum tree are uncertain, though it is thought to have originated in the Caucasus. Today, there are many plum cultivars, grown commercially for their edible fruit. The seventeenth and eighteenth century saw the development of the greengage plum in England and the Mirabelle plum in France. Dried plums or 'prunes' are produced from a family of black-skinned plums, the high sugar content of which allows them to be dried without fermenting. The best-known prune, valued for its flavour, is the prune d'Agen, named after a town in south-west France.

(TIBETAN CHERRY) FLOWERING CHERRY
PRUNUS SERRULA

The flowering cherry tree, with its brief but spectacular display of delicate pink or white spring blossom, is grown for ornamental reasons in many countries around the world. The Japanese, in particular, have a great appreciation of this tree and have developed many cultivars. Each year in Japan thousands of people celebrate spring with *hanami*, which translates as 'looking at flowers' but has come particularly to mean looking at cherry blossom, with people picnicking under the flowering trees. The Tibetan cherry is a member of the oriental cherry family and is distinctive because of its rich, red, shiny bark, so it is valued by gardeners not just for its spring blossom but for the winter colour added by its trunk.

HEIGHT: Up to 20m (66ft)
TYPE: Deciduous
BARK: Glossy, deep red with horizontal, pale fawn bands
LEAF: Narrow, oval, serrated leaves with a fine point
FLOWER: Clusters of 2–5, white to pink
FRUIT: Spherical, fleshy drupe, purple-red to black

ALMOND

PRUNUS DOLCIS

Ever since prehistoric times the almond tree has been cultivated for its edible nut and today it is grown commercially in many countries, from Portugal to Australia. Mentioned in the Bible, the almond tree was grown by the Ancient Greeks and Romans. The delicately sweet, milky white kernel has many culinary uses. Almond paste (from which marzipan is made) is employed in confectionery, while ground almonds and almond flavouring are used in baking. In Mediterranean countries sugared almonds, symbolising good luck, are traditionally given at christenings and weddings. Today the USA is the world's largest producer of almonds, followed by Spain and Italy.

HEIGHT: Up to 8m (26ft)
TYPE: Deciduous
BARK: Blackish, ruggedly cracked
LEAF: Alternate, ovate-lanceolate, finely serrated
FLOWER: Solitary or in pairs, large, pink to white
FRUIT: Oval drupe, green, leathery flesh enclosing pitted stone with edible kernel

SLOE (BLACKTHORN)

PRUNUS SPINOSA

The sloe grows wild in hedges, woodlands and wasteland and is one of Europe's most common shrubs. The specific name 'spinosa' is a reference to its spiny branches. It naturally forms dense, impenetrable thickets, providing a valuable, protective habitat for nesting and sheltering birds. Its small, blue-black berries are notoriously astringent, and were traditionally used by country people to make juice, syrup, jams, jellies and wines. In England, one popular use for sloes is to prick them then steep them in neat gin to produce aromatic, deep red-purple sloe gin. In traditional European medicine, blackthorn flowers were used to make a herbal tea, drunk as a popular tonic to cleanse the blood.

HEIGHT: Up to 5m (16ft)
TYPE: Deciduous
BARK: Dark, blackish brown
LEAF: Alternate, oval to lanceolate, dull green, finely toothed
FLOWER: Single or in pairs, white, small
FRUIT: Spherical, smooth drupe, purple to black

PRUNUS PERSICA (AMYGDALUS PERSICA) PEACH

China is the original home of the peach tree, which is thought to have been cultivated for its luscious fruit since at least the tenth century BC. From China, via trading routes such as the Silk Road, the peach spread westwards into the Middle East and Europe. The Europeans mistakenly thought that it originated from Persia, hence its specific name 'persica'. Esteemed in many countries, the peach plays a particular role in Chinese and Japanese folklore and mythology. In China it is the fruit of longevity, eaten by the immortals, while the Japanese hero Momotaro, or Peach Boy, was born inside a peach. There are two categories of peaches: clingstone and freestone, referring to how the flesh comes away from the stone. Within both categories can be found white-fleshed and yellow-fleshed fruits.

HEIGHT: Up to 8m (26ft)
TYPE: Deciduous
BARK: Dark grey, fissured when mature
LEAF: Alternate, narrow, elliptic to lanceolate, finely toothed, green
FLOWER: Borne singly or in pairs, pink
FRUIT: Large, spherical drupe with velvety or smooth skin, white flushed with pink or orange-red

PEAR
PYRUS COMMUNIS

Today's cultivated pear, widely grown for its fruit, is descended from the wild pear that is thought to have originated in the Caucasus. The fruit of the wild pear tree were small, hard, gritty and sour. Over centuries of pear-growing, however, many varieties of soft-fleshed, sweet pear were developed. In fact, there are now over 5,000 cultivated varieties of pear, among them Bartletts (popular in America), Conference and, particularly valued, Doyenne du Comice, originally grown in France. Traditionally, certain varieties of pear were considered 'cooking' pears, while others were 'eating' pears. Canning pears and drying pears are two traditional ways of preserving them.

HEIGHT: Up to 20m (66ft)
TYPE: Deciduous
BARK: Black-brown, split into small, knobbly oblongs
LEAF: Alternate, ovate to heart-shaped, glossy deep green
FLOWER: Borne in clusters, five white petals with deep pink anthers
FRUIT: Pear-shaped, fleshy, yellowish green, brown, reddish pomes, in varying sizes

(MOUNTAIN ASH) COMMON ROWAN
SORBUS AUCUPARIA

The rowan is particularly at home on high ground, where it is a pioneer tree thriving on poor or rocky soil. Featuring in Greek, Norse and Irish myths, the rowan has many folkloric beliefs attached to it. Revered by the Druids, it was long seen as a guardian tree, and was planted near homes to ward off witches or evil spirits. Similarly, sprigs of rowan were carried on journeys for protection. With its clusters of white flowers, colourful autumn foliage and orange berries, it is today valued for its ornamental qualities and widely planted in gardens, parks and streets. Its berries are much prized by birds, hence the tree's Latin name *aucuparia*, meaning 'fowler' or bird-catcher.

HEIGHT: Up to 15m (50ft)
TYPE: Deciduous
BARK: Smooth, silvery grey
LEAF: Alternate, pinnate with a terminal leaflet and two rows of long, oblong, serrated leaflets, green
FLOWER: Borne in large, flat-headed clusters, creamy-white
FRUIT: Orange-red, 1cm ($^3/_8$in) pomes

WYCH ELM
(SCOTS ELM)

ULMUS GLABRA

This hardy, woodland tree grows right across Europe, being found from Spain to Russia. However, like other elms it has suffered from Dutch Elm Disease, to which it is susceptible – though less so than the English elm. It is a tall, striking tree, with a broad crown of large leaves and a noticeably short trunk. Historically, it was valued for its strong, supple, pale-brown wood which, notably, does not decay in water and so was used for water pipes, water-wheel paddles, troughs, boat-building and sea defences. The leaves of the tree were also used to feed livestock.

HEIGHT: Up to 40m (130ft)
TYPE: Deciduous
BARK: Grey-brown
LEAF: Green, alternate, ovate, toothed at the tip, pointed
FLOWER: Borne in dense, axillary clusters, tiny with reddish anthers, petalless
FRUIT: Small, central seed surrounded by membranous wing

ENGLISH ELM
ULMUS MINOR VAR. VULGARIS
(ULMUS PROCERA)

Despite its popular name, the English elm is not native to England – although for hundreds of years its distinctive, broad shape was very much a characteristic part of the English landscape. It is now thought to have been introduced to England from the Mediterranean by the Romans, who used the tree to support grape vines. A tall, graceful tree, it was widely planted during the seventeenth and eighteenth centuries for ornamental purposes and for its timber. Valued as both durable and waterproof, elm wood was traditionally used for water pumps, ships' keels, coffins and wheels. Once widespread throughout western Europe, the English elm was devastated by a deadly disease, Dutch Elm Disease. During the 1970s the disease killed 12 million English elms, dramatically changing the English landscape.

HEIGHT: Up to 30m (100ft)
TYPE: Deciduous
BARK: Grey-brown, becoming cracked with age
LEAF: Green, alternate, ovate, double-toothed, slightly hairy underneath
FLOWER: Reddish, petalless, in clusters
FRUIT: Small, central seed, surrounded by membranous wing

BREADFRUIT ARTOCARPUS ALTILIS

HEIGHT: Up to 30m (100ft)
TYPE: Evergreen
BARK: Smooth, grey
LEAF: Alternate, large with 5–11 deeply cut lobes, glossy bright green
FLOWER: Male and female borne on same tree, in fleshy inflorescences. Male: yellowish-brown, on drooping spike; female: upright, in a rounded to oval prickly head
FRUIT: Spherical to ovoid compound fruit, often with bumpy surface, 10–30cm (4–12in) wide

Native to the Pacific islands, the breadfruit tree is now also cultivated in Africa, the Caribbean, South East Asia and Mauritius. It has long been valued for its starchy, edible fruit, which is round, green and grows as large as a man's head. There are two broad categories of breadfruit: seedless and seeded. European colonists seized upon the tree's potential as a source of cheap food for slaves and labourers, introducing it to their topical colonial territories. It was on a journey from Tahiti to the Caribbean with a thousand breadfruit plants on board that Captain William Bligh's crew on the *Bounty* famously mutinied against him. Breadfruit is harvested before it is fully ripe and is rarely eaten raw – it is usually boiled, roasted, fried or cooked in a pit. The protein-rich seeds of the seeded varieties are eaten fried or boiled.

FICUS CARICA COMMON FIG

Descended from the wild caprifig, the common fig tree has been cultivated for its soft, edible fruit for thousands of years and is now grown in many countries around the world. Cultivation of the fig is thought to have started in Egypt between 4,000 and 2,700 BC, since there is an Egyptian tomb painting showing a fig harvest, and they were prized by the Ancient Greeks and the Romans. The mature fig fruit is a botanical curiosity, being not a single fruit, as it appears, but actually hundreds of thousands of fruits, which are usually taken for seeds. The fig can be eaten either fresh or dried and there are now many cultivars grown for both purposes.

HEIGHT: Up to 10m (33ft)
TYPE: Deciduous
BARK: Grey and smooth
LEAF: Green, large, leathery, deeply lobed
FLOWER: Small, green
FRUIT: Heart-shaped, purple or green when ripe

BANYAN
FICUS BENGHALENSIS

Native to India and south-east Asia, the distinctive-looking, long-lived banyan tree is a sacred tree in both Hinduism and Buddhism and is India's national tree. The banyan tree starts life as an epiphyte, developing aerial roots that become accessory trunks, and often reaching a great size and covering large areas of ground. The world's largest banyan tree, in Calcutta's Botanical Gardens, covers some 1.6 hectares (4 acres) of land. Because of its characteristic, expanding branches it is a symbol of eternal life. In South Asian villages, large banyan trees, providing much-needed shade, were often a meeting place for villagers. The popular name comes about because of the 'banian', the Hindu traders who set up their stalls in the shelter of these shady trees.

HEIGHT: Up to 30m (100ft)
TYPE: Evergreen
BARK: Pale grey-brown
LEAF: Dark green, large, leathery, ovate with wide base
FLOWER: Male and female on same tree, tiny
FRUIT: Spherical, up to 2cm ($^7/_8$in) in diameter, scarlet when ripe

MORETON BAY FIG

FICUS MACROPHYLLA

Native to Eastern Australia, this imposing tree is named after Moreton Bay in Queensland, Australia. In rainforest conditions, it grows as a strangler fig, dropping down aerial roots which eventually kill its host tree. Often achieving a large, magnificent crown when mature, the Moreton Bay fig is supported by buttress roots and sometimes by aerial prop roots dropped down from its branches to the ground. The roots, which spread around the tree, in a scale matching the size of its crown, are surface-feeding and it is a noticeably water-hungry tree. As with other members of the fig family, it is pollinated by a specific species of wasp with which it has a symbiotic relationship. With its striking appearance, the Moreton Bay fig has been cultivated to grace avenues and parks.

HEIGHT: up to 60m (200ft)
TYPE: evergreen
BARK: grey-brown, smooth
LEAF: alternate, large, elliptic, leathery, dark green above, rusty brown beneath
FLOWER: tiny, enclosed within a fig receptacle
FRUIT: fig, ripening from green to purple

BO TREE (BODHI TREE OR PEEPUL TREE)
FICUS RELIGIOSA

HEIGHT: 15–35m
(50–115ft)
TYPE: Deciduous
BARK: Grey
LEAF: Green, alternate,
heart-shaped with a
sharp tip and slightly
wavy edges
FLOWER: Male and female
on same tree, red, tiny
FRUIT: Rounded, flat-
topped, stalkless, in
pairs, purple-brown
when ripe

Native to India and South East Asia, the broad-crowned
bo tree, sacred to both Buddhists and Hindus, is revered
as a holy tree across South Asia. In Buddhism the bo tree
is said to be the tree under which the Buddha reached
enlightenment. The bo tree, therefore, is a common
sight in Buddhist monasteries and temple grounds, and
also in Hindu temple grounds. It is a notably long-lived
tree, thought to survive for as long as 2,000 years, and is
a symbol of the continuity of life. In addition to its
religious connotations, the tree is used in Ayurvedic
medicine. Its distinctive-shaped leaves are often used as
small canvases for painting and the 'skeleton' of the
soaked leaf is used for card-making.

WHITE MULBERRY
MORUS ALBA

Native to China, the white mulberry has been cultivated for thousands of years – not for its sweet fruit but because its leaves are the preferred food of the silkworm from which silk is made. The art of silk production, or sericulture, was developed in China thousands of years ago. Chinese legend credits Lady His-Ling-Shih, wife of the Yellow Emperor who ruled China around 3,000 BC, with discovering the secrets of silkworm-rearing, and she is called the 'Goddess of Silk'. China was to keep how silk was made a closely guarded secret for many centuries and silk became a precious commodity, playing a vital part in China's economy. Today the white mulberry is still cultivated for its use in the silk trade, but is also a popular ornamental tree.

HEIGHT: Up to 14m (45ft)
TYPE: Deciduous
BARK: Pale brown to grey, ridged in maturity
LEAF: Green, glossy, smooth, rounded, toothed, alternate
FLOWER: Small, green. Male: in pendent inflorescences; female: in clusters
FRUIT: Fleshy syncarps, purple-red when ripe

BLACK MULBERRY

MORUS NIGRA

Thought to have originated in West Asia, the black mulberry tree now grows both in Europe and West Asia. It is prized for its juicy, soft, raspberry-like fruit, which, as they ripen, change colour from green to bright red to dark purple, and are notorious for staining hands and clothes blood-red. The ancient Greeks and Romans were fond of the fruit. In 1608, King James I, ruler of England, passed a decree urging the cultivation of mulberry trees in order to encourage England's silk trade. Mistakenly, however, black mulberry trees – rather than the white mulberry trees preferred by the silkworms – were widely planted, with no real gain to England's silk trade.

HEIGHT: Up to 10m (33ft)
TYPE: Deciduous
BARK: Orange-brown, scaly
LEAF: Bright green, glossy, heart-shaped, toothed
FLOWER: Small, green. Male in pendent racemes; female in clusters
FRUIT: Fleshy syncarps, purple-red when ripe

(SPANISH CHESTNUT) SWEET CHESTNUT
CASTANEA SATIVA

The sweet chestnut has flourished in southern Europe for centuries and has long been cultivated for its edible, starchy nuts, known as chestnuts. The Romans grew the tree and used its nuts for flour, a custom that still continues in southern Europe. For centuries, chestnuts were a staple food for peasants, with dried chestnuts being a useful winter food. Today, however, fresh chestnuts are something of a luxury item, traditionally associated with Christmas in Britain. French candied chestnuts, known as *marrons glacés*, are a classic treat, with their high cost reflecting the carefully controlled, time-consuming process of coating the chestnuts in several layers of sugar syrup.

HEIGHT: Up to 30m (100ft)
TYPE: Deciduous
BARK: Grey, becoming spirally fissured
LEAF: Glossy green, oblong, pointed at the tip, teethed
FLOWER: Small, pale yellow, in pendulous, spike-like catkins
FRUIT: Green, spiny husks enclosing 2–3 glossy, brown nuts

FAGUS SYLVATICA COMMON BEECH

The graceful beech tree, which grows widely throughout Europe – especially on free-draining, chalky soil – has many uses. It is thought that early books were written on thin tablets of beech wood, with the name 'beech' deriving from the Anglo-Saxon *boc*, from which came the English word 'book'. Triangular, oil-rich beech nuts, known as 'mast', were historically an important food for pigs, which would be encouraged to forage in beech woods, and the nuts were also used to feed herds of park deer. The tough wood of the beech tree has traditionally been used for furniture and flooring, while the fact that it retains its brown leaves for a long time has made it popular for hedging. In the autumn, beech woods are traditionally a fruitful place in which to look for wild mushrooms.

HEIGHT: Up to 40m (130ft)
TYPE: Deciduous
BARK: Silver-grey, smooth
LEAF: Green, ovate, wavy edge
FLOWER: Male: yellow in pendulous clusters; female: inconspicuous in leaf axils
FRUIT: Prickly husks containing one or two, three-sided, brown nuts

(COMMON/PEDUNCULATE OAK) ENGLISH OAK
QUERCUS ROBUR

A long-living tree, capable of living for hundreds of years, the English oak has long been revered. It features in Greek and Norse myths and the Bible and was also worshipped by the druids. In practical terms, the oak has historically been much valued for its strong, durable timber; for centuries, the ships in the English Royal Navy were built out of sturdy oak. The bark, with its high tannin content, was used by the tanning industry, while acorns, the fruit of the oak tree, provided valuable food for pigs. Oak trees, especially mature ones, play an important part in the forest's ecosystem, providing food and shelter for many creatures from insects to birds as well as animals such as squirrels.

HEIGHT: 40m (130ft)
TYPE: Deciduous
BARK: Pale grey with deep ridges
LEAF: Green with irregular deep lobes
FLOWER: Male: drooping catkins; female: inconspicuous, on short stalks
FRUIT: Ovoid, long-stalked nuts, one-third to one-half enclosed in a cup

SESSILE OAK (DURMAST OAK) QUERCUS PETRAEA

HEIGHT: 25–40m (82–130ft)
TYPE: Deciduous
BARK: Grey-brown, fissured
LEAF: Glossy, green, with regular, shallow lobes on a long stalk
FLOWER: Male: in catkins; female: on short stalks
FRUIT: Ovoid nuts, in stalkless clusters

Native to Europe, this impressive, slow-growing, long-lived tree has a number of historic uses. Its common name derives from the fact that its acorns are stalkless (sessile), growing directly on the tree's twigs. Its timber, which is finer-grained and less tough than that of the common oak, has a number of uses, including veneer, poles, fencing, wine barrels and building timber. The tannin in its wood meant that it was traditionally used for tanning leather. Like the common oak, it is an important tree ecologically, providing food and shelter for a range of insects, birds and mammals. Late to leaf, it allows a lot of light to reach the ground, permitting a range of flora to flourish beneath its branches.

QUERCUS SUBER CORK OAK

Native to the Mediterranean region, the venerable cork oak has long been cultivated for its thick, spongy bark from which cork is made. Remarkably, the cork oak can withstand major stripping of its bark, simply renewing it within a few years. In countries such as Portugal and Spain the cork forests are carefully managed, with trees harvested of their bark every 9–12 years, and they play an important part in the local economy. Cork's best-known use has been as a bottle stopper, with 15 billion cork stoppers produced each year. Today, however, the rise in popularity of plastic stoppers is threatening the economic viability of these unique cork forests and consequently the wildlife (much of it already endangered) that lives there.

HEIGHT: Up to 20m (66ft)
TYPE: Evergreen
BARK: Grey to orange, thick, ridged bark
LEAF: Dark glossy green, ovate to oblong, toothed, alternate
FLOWER: Male and female on same tree. Male: in slender catkins; female: on short, downy stalks
FRUIT: Ovoid nut, enclosed halfway in cup

COMMON ALDER
(BLACK ALDER)
ALNUS GLUTINOSA

Found throughout Europe and western Asia, the alder is known as a water-loving tree, preferring damp environments such as marshes or land by lakes or rivers. It is a fast-growing, pioneer species, living only up to 150 years. There are many mythic and folkloric references to the alder tree and it has many traditional medicinal uses. Over the centuries, alder wood, which takes on an attractive reddish colour when cut, has had a number of uses, from charcoal for gunpowder to clog-making. Alder wood's particular quality, however, is that it does not rot when immersed in water and so it has been used extensively for boats, locks and water pipes. Most famously, the city of Venice is supported on foundations made from alder pilings.

HEIGHT: Up to 25m (82ft)
TYPE: Deciduous
BARK: Dark grey-brown, scaly when mature
LEAF: Green, rounded, finely toothed, alternate
FLOWER: Male and female on same tree. Male: reddish brown, in dropping catkins; female: red, solitary
FRUIT: Woody, oval, cone-like

SILVER BIRCH
BETULA PENDULA

Despite its dainty appearance, the silver birch can withstand both severe cold and drought and is consequently found throughout Europe and in western and northern Asia. A fast-growing and prolific seeding tree, the silver birch can establish itself very quickly, but it is also short-lived. Its timber is too soft for use in the construction trade but is used for furniture and coopering. Its distinctive fine-twigged branches (which droop downwards, giving silver birches their distinctive 'weeping' look) are traditionally used to make besom brooms, popular with gardeners. The papery bark, impermeable to water, was used for roofing and to make containers. Its graceful shape and distinctive white trunk have meant that the silver birch is a tree valued for its ornamental appearance and it is widely planted in parks and gardens.

HEIGHT: 30m (100ft)
TYPE: Deciduous
BARK: Silvery white with black fissures
LEAF: Green, triangular with toothed edges
FLOWER: Male and female catkins, borne on the same tree. Male: yellow, drooping; female: green, upright, later pendulous
FRUIT: Winged seeds, borne in catkins

HORNBEAM
CARPINUS BETULUS

Found in Europe and south-western Asia, the hornbeam is a hardy tree, thriving particularly in richer soil. Its name 'hornbeam', derived from Old English, means 'hard tree' – a reference to its extremely tough wood. Traditionally, its hard, white timber was particularly used for ox yokes, butchers' blocks, tools and mill cogs, while the tree was often coppiced for charcoal production. Like beech, which it closely resembles, it is a popular tree for hedging, retaining its leaves even after they have changed colour in autumn.

HEIGHT: Up to 30m (100ft)
TYPE: Deciduous
BARK: Silver-grey, smooth
LEAF: Dark green, oval, double-toothed
Flower: Male and female catkins on same tree. Male: axillary; female: at tips of shoots
FRUIT: Ribbed nut, held in a three-lobed bract

HAZEL

CORYLUS AVELLANA

This shrubby, short-lived tree is found throughout Europe, western Asia and North Africa, thriving in woodlands and hedges. Its ability to produce multiple stems gives hazel a characteristic dense appearance and it has long been extensively used for coppicing. Hazel stems, which can be split lengthways and bent back on themselves, were historically used for weaving into wattle hurdles and to make hoops for baskets. In Celtic mythology hazel is associated with wisdom and it is traditionally used for divining. Valued too for its edible nuts, known as hazelnuts, it has long been cultivated, with a number of cultivars now in existence.

HEIGHT: Up to 15m (50ft)
TYPE: Deciduous
BARK: Silver grey to pale brown, sometimes peeling
LEAF: Green, nearly round, double-toothed
FLOWER: Male and female on same tree. Male: long catkins; female: small, bud-like with red stigmas
FRUIT: Nut surrounded by a bract-like husk

PECAN
CARYA ILLINOINENSIS

A member of the hickory family, native to North America's southern states, the pecan tree is the USA's best-known native nut. The name pecan comes from the Algonquin Indian *paccan*. The kernel of the nut, housed in a characteristic smooth, red-brown, thin shell, resembles that of a walnut, but has a sweeter, milder, buttery flavour. A significant breakthrough in cultivating pecans came about in 1845 when Antoine, an African-American slave gardener, successfully grafted wild pecans onto cultivated stock, increasing productivity. The commercial cultivation of pecans began in North America in the 1880s and there are now hundreds of varieties. Today, the USA produces between 80–95% of the world's pecan crop, though it is also cultivated in other countries, including Australia and South Africa. The nuts are much used in confectionery and desserts, most famously in pecan pie.

HEIGHT: 30–55m (100–180ft)
TYPE: Deciduous
BARK: Pale grey-brown, deeply fissured and ridged
LEAF: Alternate, pinnate, 9–17 lanceolate, coarsely toothed, green leaflets
FLOWER: Petalless; male: axillary, pendulous catkins; female: stalkless in terminal spikes
FRUIT: Oval, brown-shelled nut, borne singly or in groups, up to 6cm (2in) long, inside husk

JUGLANS REGIA WALNUT

This handsome, wide-spreading tree is found from Europe through to China, with the Romans credited with spreading the tree throughout Europe from the Middle East. It has long been cultivated for its edible, protein-rich nuts, eaten in their own right and also pressed for their oil. The distinctive brain shape of the kernel meant that the Romans and Greeks believed it was effective in treating headaches. Pickled walnuts are a traditional British condiment, while the French use walnut oil for salad dressings. The walnut tree has also long been cultivated for its fine-grained, dark wood, which is particularly valued for high-quality furniture and coach panels.

HEIGHT: Up to 30m (100ft)
TYPE: Deciduous
BARK: Silvery grey, deeply fissured when mature
LEAF: Dark green, leathery, shiny, pinnate with 5–9 ovate to elliptic leaflets, distinctive shoe-polish smell when crushed
FLOWER: Small, petalless male and female flowers on the same tree. Male: in axillary, pendulous catkins; female: stalkless
FRUIT: Round, brown-shelled nut, borne singly or in pairs, up to 5cm (2in) long, inside husk

PAPAYA

CARICA PAPAYA

Tthe papaya is widely grown throughout the tropics for its large, soft-fleshed fruit. It is a fast-growing tree, easily grown from seed, and bears fruit within a year. There are several varieties of papaya available, ranging from those bearing pear-shaped fruit, weighing around 500g (1lb) to those producing large rounded papayas, weighing as much as 9kg (20lb). The raw papaya fruit and its leaves contain a powerful digestive enzyme, papain, which is traditionally used to tenderise tough meat. Ripe papaya fruit, with their yellow, orange or pink flesh, are a traditional breakfast in the tropics, eaten with a squeeze of fresh lime juice to cut through the sweetness.

HEIGHT: 2–10m (6–33ft)
TYPE: Evergreen
BARK: Light brown, with leaf scars evident
LEAF: Alternate, long, deeply lobed, dark green
FLOWER: Males and females on separate trees, with pale yellow or pink petals. Male: in pendent panicles; female: solitary or in small clusters
FRUIT: Large, ovoid, fleshy fruit up to 30cm (12in) long, with orange, yellow or pink flesh surrounding multiple soft, black seeds

BAOBAB

ADANSONIA DIGITATA

This remarkable African tree has a striking appearance, easily identified by its a huge, swollen trunk in which the baobab stores water to cope with the arid conditions in which it grows. It is sometimes nicknamed the 'upside-down tree' because its branches are said to resemble roots. A slow-growing tree, the baobab is rumoured to live for many centuries though the fact that it does not produce annual growth rings has made it difficult to prove this scientifically. In Africa the tree has many traditional uses. Its fruit and leaves are edible, rainwater is found in the clefts of its branches and its fibrous bark is stripped and used for fishing nets and mats — with the tree able to survive ring-barking. Its large, white, strongly scented flowers attract the bats that pollinate it.

HEIGHT: 10–25m (33–82ft)
TYPE: Deciduous
BARK: Grey-brown
LEAF: Dark green, glossy, hand-like with 5–7 long leaflets
FLOWER: Solitary, axillary, large, sweet-scented, with white to cream petals
FRUIT: Ovoid, brown, hairy capsule, black seeds

ANNATTO (ACHIOTE) BIXA ORELLANA

HEIGHT: 3–10m (10–33ft)
TYPE: Evergreen
BARK: Light brown,
fissured when mature
LEAF: Alternate, ovate to
heart-shaped, light
green with prominent
veins
FLOWER: Large, terminal
panicles, 5–7 obovate,
pinkish petals
FRUIT: Flattened, ovate
capsule with bristles,
containing bright red
seeds

Native to tropical America, the annatto tree has long
been used for the red colouring derived from its scarlet
seeds. The colour derives from a carotene pigment
known as bixene and historically it was used by tribal
people as both a body paint and a fabric dye. Europe,
during the seventeenth and nineteenth centuries, saw
annatto gaining popularity as a food colouring – in
England it was used to add a rich orange colour to
Cheshire cheese and red Leicester. Anatto oil or lard,
derived from the orange-red pulp around the seeds, is
used to add colour to a number of Caribbean dishes,
such as codfish cakes. Ground annatto seeds are used as
a spice in Mexico. This pretty flowering tree is also
popularly grown as an ornamental tree in the tropics.

THEOBROMA CACAO (CACAO) COCOA

Native to Latin America, this evergreen tree is now cultivated in many tropical countries around the world, with West Africa a major grower. The reason for this interest is the tree's large cocoa pods, the raw material from which chocolate is made. The tree's Latin name reflects the historic allure of chocolate, with Linnaeus calling it 'the food of the gods'. The Maya, whose civilisation flowered in the first millennium AD, drank a drink made from chocolate. Today, the process of making chocolate sees the seeds of the cocoa pod scooped out, fermented and dried, before shelling, roasting and processing to extract the cocoa butter and cocoa solids.

HEIGHT: Up to 10m (33ft)
TYPE: Evergreen
BARK: Dark brown, fissured
LEAF: Dark green, leathery, large, elliptic to oblong
FLOWER: Borne singly or in groups, white to pink
FRUIT: Ovoid, furrowed pod, yellow to reddish

TILIA X EUROPAEA (LINDEN) COMMON LIME

A naturally occurring hybrid between the broad and small-leaved limes, this tall tree is found throughout Europe. It is widely cultivated and planted along high streets or avenues. In fact, two aspects of the common lime make it an unlikely choice for street planting: the first is the unsightly suckers that it produces prolifically at its base; the second is the fact that it attracts aphids, which drop sticky secretions that are a particular annoyance for car owners. On the plus side, its tiny flowers have an exquisite fragrance, which perfumes the air. These flowers are a firm favourite with bees, and linden honey is much valued. Dried linden flowers are used by the French for a popular tisane, which is utilised as an antispasmodic. The lime tree's soft, white, close-grained wood is traditionally used for fine carving.

HEIGHT: Up to 40m (130ft)
TYPE: Deciduous
BARK: Grey to grey-brown, shallowly fissured when mature
LEAF: Green, heart-shaped with a tapering tip
FLOWER: Pale yellow-green with pale green bracts at base, in clusters, fragrant
FRUIT: Woody, rounded drupe, covered with grey-brown hairs

SYCAMORE
ACER PSEUDOPLATANUS

The largest member of the European maple family is found throughout most of western Europe and is one of the most common northern temperate trees. It is a tough tree able to withstand exposure, pollution and salt-laden winds, making it a useful windbreak tree for upland farms and coastal areas. So successful is it at colonising open ground that it is regarded as an invasive species in some areas. Its winged pairs of seeds or 'keys' spiral downwards in a distinctive 'helicopter'-like fashion, playing an important part in spreading the tree. Its hard, strong, creamy-white timber, although not durable out of doors, is particularly valued for flooring, furniture-making and joinery.

HEIGHT: Up to 40m (130ft)
TYPE: Deciduous
BARK: Grey-pink
LEAF: Green, palmate with 5 toothed lobes
FLOWER: Borne in pendulous clusters, green
FRUIT: Winged keys arranged in pairs

JAPANESE MAPLE
ACER PALMATUM

Native to China, Japan, Korea and Taiwan,
the dainty Japanese maple has been
cultivated in Japan for centuries, long
valued for its attractive, colourful foliage
and also a popular bonsai tree. Its specific
name is a reference to the tree's distinctive
hand-shaped leaves. Introduced to Europe in
1820, the Japanese maple is now available in
hundreds of different cultivars, varying in
leaf colour (from green and yellow to red
and purple), leaf shape and leaf size,
Japanese maples with red-coloured leaves
being especially popular. The tree's graceful
shape combined with its striking foliage has
made it an extremely popular ornamental
tree, widely planted in gardens and parks.

HEIGHT: Up to 15m (50ft)
TYPE: Deciduous
BARK: Brown-grey, smooth with pale longitudinal stripes
LEAF: Opposite, palmate with 5-9 deep, finely serrated
lobes
FLOWER: Deep red in small spreading heads
FRUIT: Red winged keys, in pairs

SUGAR MAPLE

ACER SACCHARUM

North America's largest maple is famous as the source of maple syrup, which is made from the sap of this large, attractive tree. It is Canada's national tree, with a bright red maple leaf adorning the country's flag. Tapping the maple for its sap was a process known to the Native Americans and subsequently the North American settlers. The maple tree is able to withstand the process of tapping, in which gallons of its sap are drained away. The tapping process takes place during late winter to early spring and one tree can produce several gallons. However, 182 litres (40 gallons) of sap are needed to produce 4.5 litres (1 gallon) of maple syrup, hence its high cost. In addition to its valuable sap, the sugar maple is prized for its fine timber. With its striking autumn colours, it is also planted in parks and gardens for ornamental reasons.

HEIGHT: 30–36m (100–120ft)
TYPE: Deciduous
BARK: Grey-brown, scaly when mature
LEAF: Dark green with 5 palmate, notched lobes
FLOWER: Small, greenish yellow
FRUIT: Winged keys, arranged in pairs

AESCULUS HIPPOCASTANUM HORSE CHESTNUT

Native to the Balkans, the splendid horse chestnut, with its attractive, eye-catching 'candles' of creamy white blossom, became a popular ornamental tree during the seventeenth century, when it was widely planted throughout Europe along avenues and in churchyards and parks. There is some mystery as to how it came by its name. One theory is that the nuts, though inedible to humans, were used for horse fodder. Another is that the leaf scars on twigs resemble horseshoes. In herbal medicine, horse chestnut is used to treat varicose veins and haemorrhoids. For centuries in Britain its large, shiny nuts, which grow encased in spiny cases, have been collected by children and used to play a game called 'conkers' in which the threaded nuts are smashed against each other.

HEIGHT: Up to 40m (130ft)
TYPE: Deciduous
BARK: Dark brown, coarsely scaly when mature
LEAF: Large, green, palmate, with 5 to 7 leaflets
FLOWER: White or pink, borne in upright panicles
FRUIT: Green, spiky, spherical husks, each containing a glossy brown seed or seeds

FRANKINCENSE BOSWELLIA SACRA

HEIGHT: Up to 5m (16ft)
TYPE: Deciduous
BARK: Orange-brown, papery, peeling
LEAF: Alternate, pinnate with a terminal leaflet and 6–8 pairs of obovate-oblong green leaves
FLOWER: Borne in axillary racemes at the ends of branches, small, white to pink
FRUIT: Small, ovoid, green drupe

Native to the dry regions of North East Africa and Southern Arabia, the low-growing frankincense tree has long been valued for its aromatic gum resin, formerly worth its weight in gold. The resin has been harvested for centuries by nomadic tribes who visit the trees to make small cuts in their trunks, returning a few weeks later to collect the 'tears' of resin that have seeped out and solidified. In this way, each tree can yield several kilograms of resin in a year. Frankincense was used by the Ancient Egyptians in their religious rites and to anoint the mummies of their kings, with incense containing frankincense found in King Tutankhamun's tomb. It was a traditional incense in Judaism and is still used as a fragrant incense by Catholics and the Coptic church.

ANARCARDIUM OCCIDENTALE CASHEW

Thought to be native to Brazil, the cashew tree is cultivated throughout the tropics for its valuable nuts. The Portuguese introduced the cashew tree from Brazil to the East Indies, from where its cultivation spread to India. The kidney-shaped cashew nut itself is contained in a husk that has an extremely acrid sap, making extracting the nut a challenging process. Usually, the husk is roasted until it can be cracked open without damaging the nut inside. Roasted cashews are a popular appetiser in North America, Europe and the Middle East, while in India freshly fried cashews, spiced with black pepper or chilli powder, are traditionally served with drinks. Cashew nuts are also used in cookery, in dishes such as Chinese stir-fried chicken with cashews.

HEIGHT: 4–12m (13–40ft)
TYPE: Evergreen
BARK: Grey-brown, fissured with age
LEAF: Alternate, obovate to oblong, leathery, mid-green
FLOWER: Borne in terminal panicle, with yellow-green to pink petals
FRUIT: Nut at the end of a fleshy, red, pear-shaped stalk

MANGIFERA INDICA MANGO

The mango tree has been cultivated for its fruit in India since at least 2000 BC and is today widely grown in tropical countries around the world. The fruit is prized for the orange, juicy flesh with its distinctive flavour and it has much mythology and folklore attached to it; for example, the mango features in an Indian Vedic legend, associated with love. For centuries in India it was a luxury, with only rajas and nawabs allowed to grow mango orchards. Today there are over 1,000 cultivars, one of the most highly valued being the succulent Alphonso mango from India. In addition to being eaten raw when ripe, green mangoes are traditionally used in India to make chutneys and pickles. Sour green mangoes are also used in spicy salads in Thailand. Drying and canning are both popular ways of preserving the fruit.

HEIGHT: 10–45m (33–148ft)
TYPE: Evergreen
BARK: Greyish brown, smooth, becoming scaly and furrowed with age
LEAF: Alternate, narrowly elliptic to lanceolate, leathery, dark green
FLOWER: Terminal panicles, tiny, pink, yellow, green, brown or white
FRUIT: Fleshy drupe, varying in size and colour

MASTIC

PISTACIA LENTISCUS

Native to the Mediterranean region, this small tree has long been valued for its clear, sticky resin, also known as 'mastic', which it exudes when its bark is cut. This resin was used medicinally in ancient times to treat gastro-intestinal conditions and coughs. In its natural form, mastic was also chewed to strengthen the gums and to sweeten the breath. In Greek and Turkish cuisines, it has traditionally added flavour to confectionery (including Turkish delight), ice cream, bread and alcoholic drinks. A large propotion of the world's supply of mastic is gathered from the Greek island of Chios, with incisions made in the stems of mastic trees and the resulting 'tears' of resin harvested.

HEIGHT: 2.4–3.6m (8–12ft)
TYPE: Evergreen
BARK: Grey-brown, becoming rough with scaly plates
LEAF: Alternate, pinnate, 4–10 oblong-lanceolate, green leaflets
FLOWER: Males and females on separate trees, yellowish-white with red stamens and stigmas
FRUIT: Spherical drupes, red ripening to black

NEEM

AZADIRACHTA INDICA

Indigenous to India, this fast-growing, hardy, evergreen tree has been valued for its medicinal properties on the Indian sub-continent for thousands of years. Used extensively in Ayurvedic medicine, the neem tree possesses notable antimicrobial properties. Various parts of the neem tree are used for toothpastes, cosmetics and insect repellents and medicinally to treat infections, skin conditions and to reduce swellings Neem oil, extracted from its seeds, is its most important product. Such are the neem tree's properties that it is the subject of attempts to patent its extracts. Its uses are not only medicinal: its heavy wood, which repels pests such as termites, is popular for furniture, its bark is used for fibre and it is also planted along roadsides to provide shade.

HEIGHT: 20–35m (66–115ft)
TYPE: Evergreen
BARK: Grey-black, rough
LEAF: Glossy green, alternate, pinnate with toothed, sickle-shaped leaflets having a characteristic scent when rubbed
FLOWER: Borne in axillary inflorescences, white, fragrant
FRUIT: Single-seeded drupe, yellow when ripe, up to 2cm ($^7/_8$in) long

MAHOGANY SWIETENIA MAHAGONI

HEIGHT: Up to 20m (66ft)
TYPE: Deciduous
BARK: Dark reddish brown, scaly
LEAF: Dark green, alternate, pinnate with 5 to 7 pairs of ovate leaflets
FLOWER: Panicles, greenish yellow
FRUIT: Woody, oblong capsule with winged seeds

The best known of all tropical hardwoods, mahogany grows in the West Indies, Bahamas and Southern Florida. This slow-growing, long-lived tree has been valued for centuries for its hard, close-grained timber, which has a distinctive red-brown hue. From the sixteenth century, mahogany timber was carried to Europe for use in the furniture trade, and the acclaimed cabinet-maker Thomas Chippendale famously used it for many pieces. Over the centuries the mahogany tree has been felled in such large numbers that there are very few now left in the wild and it is officially an endangered species. One of the largest mahogany trees still surviving is found in Florida's Everglades National Park in the USA.

DIOSPYROS EBENUM EBONY

Found in India and Sri Lanka, this slow-growing, evergreen tree is valued for its distinctive heartwood, known as ebony. This intensely black, fine-grained wood, so dense that it sinks in water, has been valued since the the time of the Ancient Egyptians. Historical uses for ebony include finely carved cabinets, the black chess pieces in chess sets and the black piano and harpsichord keys. The popularity of its timber means that the tree is now extremely rare.

HEIGHT: Up to 30m (100ft)
TYPE: Evergreen
BARK: Dark grey, flaking in rectangular pieces
LEAF: Bright green, alternate, oblong-elliptic
FLOWER: Male and female on separate trees. Male: yellowish with white corolla, borne in clusters; female: yellowish-white, solitary
FRUIT: Large, spherical to ovoid berry

LEMON

CITRUS X LIMON

This small, evergreen tree is thought to have originated in east Asia and been introduced to the Mediterranean towards the end of the first century. It has long been grown for its juicy, yellow-skinned fruits, with the Arabs credited with spreading lemon cultivation through the Mediterranean region. Throughout the Middle Ages lemons were an exotic and expensive novelty in Europe, but over the centuries they became more widely used. The Spanish introduced them to the New World in the fifteenth century and today California is a leading producer of lemons. High in vitamin C, the lemon adds its distinctive sourness to beverages (such as lemonade) and dishes of all kinds.

HEIGHT: 3–6m (10–20ft)
TYPE: Evergreen
BARK: Grey-brown
LEAF: Glossy green, alternate, elliptic-ovate, toothed
FLOWER: Axillary, solitary or in clusters, white
FRUIT: Ovoid, yellow when ripe

(SEVILLE ORANGE) BITTER ORANGE
CITRUS AURANTIUM

Thought to originate in south-western China, the bitter orange was introduced westwards by Arab traders; it was cultivated particularly in Sicily at the beginning of the eleventh century AD and around Seville in Spain by the end of the twelfth century. It was grown for its fragrant, round, orange-coloured fruit, though gradually the sweet orange (*Citrus sinensis*) became more widely cultivated. Today, the best-known use of the bitter orange is for marmalade, the characteristic British jam made from these aromatic fruit – bitter oranges make the best marmalade, giving not only the requisite sharp taste but also a particular citrus flavour.

HEIGHT: Up to 10m (33ft)
TYPE: Evergreen
BARK: Green to grey-brown
LEAF: Alternate, ovate to oblong, smooth, glossy green
FLOWER: Solitary or in short, axillary racemes, white, fragrant
FRUIT: Spherical fruit, greenish yellow to orange

ARGAN

ARGANIA SPINOSA

Unique to Morocco, this small, long-living, thorny tree thrives in arid conditions, tolerating poor soil, and plays an important role in rural Moroccan life. Found only in the south-west of Morocco, between Essaouira and Agadir, the argan forests provide food for goats, which climb up the trees' gnarled trunks to eat their leaves and fruit. The tree is also the source of argan oil, a valuable commodity, which is obtained by crushing the argan nuts, a process traditionally carried out by various women's co-operatives. The resulting oil, which has a distinctive nutty flavour and contains 80 per cent unsaturated fatty acids, is historically a luxury condiment and is used as a flavouring rather than a cooking oil. Recently argan oil has been finding a market outside Morocco, increasing hopes that the diminishing argan forests may find protection for economic reasons.

HEIGHT: Up to 8–10m (26–33ft)
TYPE: Evergreen
BARK: Grey-brown, cracked
LEAF: Green, alternate, lanceolate-oblong
FLOWER: Axillary clusters, greenish white
FRUIT: Green to brown, ovoid berry

QUININE CINCHONA CALISAYA

HEIGHT: Up to 25m (82ft)
TYPE: Evergreen
BARK: Grey-brown
LEAF: Green, shiny, opposite, elliptic to oblong
FLOWER: Terminal panicles, tubular, white to pink, fragrant
FRUIT: Ovoid capsule, 1.5cm (½in) long, containing winged seeds

Native to South America, the quinine tree gained fame as the 'fever tree', with its bitter, powdered bark an effective treatment for malaria when none other existed. Legend has it that the Countess of Chinchona, wife of the Spanish Viceroy of Peru, fell ill with malaria in 1638 and was saved by being treated by Peruvians with quinine bark, news of which she subsequently spread to Europe. Much secrecy surrounded quinine bark, known as 'Jesuits' bark', and the Peruvians tightly controlled supply of this valuable drug. During the 1860s, however, quinine trees were successfully introduced to Java by the British and the Dutch, which subsequently became a major source of the medicine. Another well-known use of quinine was as a flavouring for tonic water, with gin and tonic traditionally drunk to fend off fevers.

COFFEA ARABICA ARABICA COFFEE

Originally from Africa, the Arabica coffee tree is now cultivated in many tropical countries around the world, grown for its caffeine-rich beans. Its origins, according to folklore, are that a goatherd in Ethiopia noticed that his flock were particularly lively after chewing the berries of a particular tree and sampled the beans for himself, so discovering coffee. Coffee-drinking became popular throughout the Middle East and was introduced to Europe by Venetian traders in the early seventeenth century. This exotic, bitter drink, with its stimulating effects, soon became hugely fashionable. Today, coffee beans are a commodity traded on the international markets, with Arabica beans (as opposed to beans from the Robusta coffee tree) seen as the premium coffee bean.

HEIGHT: 4–5m (13–16ft)
TYPE: Evergreen
BARK: Brown, finely fissured
LEAF: Dark green, glossy, opposite, ovate to elliptic
FLOWER: Borne in clusters of 5–20 with five white petals, fragrant
FRUIT: Ovoid berry, red when ripe

ASH

FRAXINUS EXCELSIOR

This tall, fast-growing, deciduous tree, with its distinctive sooty black buds, grows widely across Europe on a wide range of soils. Its winged seeds, known as ash keys, spin well and are widely dispersed by the wind, aiding the ash tree's distribution. In Norse mythology the first man was made from ash and Yggdrasil, the tree of the world, is thought to be an ash tree. In British folklore, the ash is credited with protective properties. Its strong, flexible wood has many traditional uses, including the manufacture of joists, beams, tool handles, sports equipment and horse shafts and for carriage building.

HEIGHT: Up to 45m (148ft)
TYPE: Deciduous
BARK: Grey-brown, fissured when mature
LEAF: Green, pinnate with 7–15 ovate-oblong leaflets
FLOWER: Small, purplish, in short, axillary clusters
FRUIT: Winged keys, in clusters, glossy green, turning brown

OLEA EUROPAEA OLIVE

This low-growing, long-lived, evergreen tree has long been cultivated in the Mediterranean region for the precious oil obtained by pressing the fruit of the tree; references to olive oil have been found on Cretan tablets dating back to 2,500 BC. In Greek mythology the olive tree was a gift to the Greeks from the goddess Athena and both the Greeks and the Romans valued the tree highly. There are many references to it in the Bible, where it is mentioned as an anointing oil. Today, the olive tree's gnarled shape and silvery leaves are a characteristic sight of the Mediterranean region although it is also grown in other parts of the world, including South America, Australia and South Africa.

HEIGHT: Up to 15m (50ft)
TYPE: Evergreen
BARK: Grey with gnarled ridges
LEAF: Dark green above, silver-grey beneath, opposite, leathery, lanceolate or ovate
FLOWER: Borne in axillary clusters, small, white
FRUIT: Ovoid drupe, green turning to black

INDIAN BEAN
CATALPA BIGNONIOIDES

Native to the south-eastern states of the United States, from Georgia to Florida and across to Mississippi, the popular name 'Indian bean' is said to refer to the fact that the bean-shaped bean pods of the tree were used by the Native Americans. Its Latin name *catalpa* is reputedly a mispronunciation of 'catawba', the name of the Native American tribe in whose territory European botanists first found it. It is an attractive, exotic-looking tree, with large, heart-shaped leaves and abundant clusters of white, bell-shaped blossoms in the spring, followed by the distinctive long seed pods. Consequently, it is widely planted as an ornamental tree both in America and also in Britain, where it was introduced in the eighteenth century and can still be found adorning parks, squares and gardens.

HEIGHT: Up to 18m (60ft)
TYPE: Deciduous
BARK: Orange to pink-brown, scaly
LEAF: Bright green, heart-shaped, tapering to a sharp point, unlobed or shallowly lobed
FLOWER: Panicles, trumpet-shaped, up to 5cm (2in) long, white, with yellow and purple spots
FRUIT: Pendulous seedpods, 40cm (16in) long

JACARANDA
JACARANDA MIMOSIFOLIA

Native to South America, this blue-flowering jacaranda is the best-known member of the jacaranda genus which contains around 40 species. Today it can be found in tropical and sub-tropical countries around the world, including Australia and South Africa. A fast-growing tree, it has a beautiful, eye-catching, long-lasting display of purplish blue flowers and is consequently a popular ornamental tree, planted to line streets and avenues and in parks. So many jacaranda trees have been planted in the streets of Pretoria, South Africa, that it is known as 'Jacaranda City'. In Australia, where the tree flowers in December, it is associated with Christmas.

HEIGHT: 5–15m (16–50ft)
TYPE: Deciduous
BARK: Grey-brown, smooth when young, finely scaled when mature
LEAF: Opposite, bipinnate, with 13–41 green leaflets
FLOWER: Purplish blue, tubular, in terminal panicles
FRUIT: Oval, woody seed pods, containing winged seeds

SAUSAGE TREE KIGELIA AFRICANA

HEIGHT: 10–15m (33–50ft)
TYPE: Deciduous
BARK: Grey-brown, rough
LEAF: Opposite, pinnate, with 3–6 pairs of elliptic to lanceolate, green leaflets
FLOWER: Dark red to purple, bell-shaped, in panicles
FRUIT: Pendulous, grey-green, sausage-shaped capsules

Native to Africa, the sausage tree is easily identified by its large, heavy, salami-like fruits, which hang down from its branches on long stalks and explain its common English name. Its generic name 'kigelia' is derived from the Bantu name for the tree *kigeli keia*. Its strongly scented flowers open only at night and are pollinated by bats, who visit them to gather pollen and nectar. The fruits of the tree are used in traditional African herbal medicine to treat various ailments including abscesses, rheumatism and venereal disease, and are also used in brewing beer. Its tough wood is traditionally used to make dugout canoes.

TECTONA GRANDIA TEAK

This tall, long-lived tree, native to Asia and South East Asia, has long been valued for its dark brown timber, which is both extremely durable and easily worked. High in natural oils, teak wood is very resistant to both insects and the effects of weather, making it a traditional choice for boat decks and high-quality garden furniture. In India it is valued for the fact that it is resistant to termites and so it is used for doors and window frames. It is a very long-lived tree, with one venerable specimen in Thailand thought to have lived for over 1,000 years. Because of its valuable timber it has been extensively harvested in the wild and is increasingly cultivated in plantations.

HEIGHT: Up to 50m (165ft)
TYPE: Deciduous
BARK: Pale brown, flaky in strips
LEAF: Dark green opposite, large, ovate
FLOWER: Borne in pyramidal inflorescences, white
FRUIT: Inflated calyx surrounding a stone containing seeds

HOLLY

ILEX AQUIFOLIUM

Native to Europe and West Asia, the
evergreen holly is a shade-tolerant tree,
able to survive as an understory species in
woodlands, particularly oak and beech
woods. With its glossy green leaves and
striking, bright red berries, the holly has
long been a symbol of life and renewal,
featuring in pagan mid-winter festivals –
although today it is widely associated with
Christmas. There is much folklore associated
with it and it was long considered unlucky
to cut down a holly tree. Another popular
belief is that the quantity of berries it bears
predicts whether or not there is a harsh
winter to come – plentiful berries indicate
severe weather ahead. Its berries, in
addition to providing garden colour, are an
important winter foodstuff for birds. Its
heavy, fine-grained wood was used for
billiard cues, chess pieces, printing blocks
and horsewhips.

HEIGHT: Up to 20m (66ft)
TYPE: Evergreen
BARK: Brownish grey
LEAF: Dark green, glossy, ovate, some with spines, some
without
FLOWER: Male and female on separate trees, borne in
axillary clusters, small, white, sometimes purple-
tinged
FRUIT: Round, shiny, red berries, borne in clusters

SAMBUCUS NIGRA ELDER

Found throughout Europe, the elder is a widespread tree, usually growing naturally rather than deliberately cultivated. It is rapid-growing, able to thrive on wasteland, and easily distinguished in the spring by its flat-topped heads of tiny, creamy white flowers. In British folklore it is considered a lucky tree, offering protection against evil spirits, and it also had many traditional medicinal uses. Today, however, its best-known use is as the source of elderflower cordial, a sweet syrup flavoured with its fragrant flowers, which was once a traditional country drink but is now manufactured on a commercial scale. Elderflower 'champagne', made by fermenting the flowerheads, was another farmhouse beverage, as was elderberry wine, which is made from the purple-black berries.

HEIGHT: Up to 10m (33ft)
TYPE: Deciduous
BARK: Creamy grey with criss-cross ridges
LEAF: Green, opposite, pinnate with a terminal leaflet, 5–7 leaflets
FLOWER: Borne in terminal, flat panicles, small, creamy white, fragrant
FRUIT: Purple-black drupes up to 6mm (¼in) wide

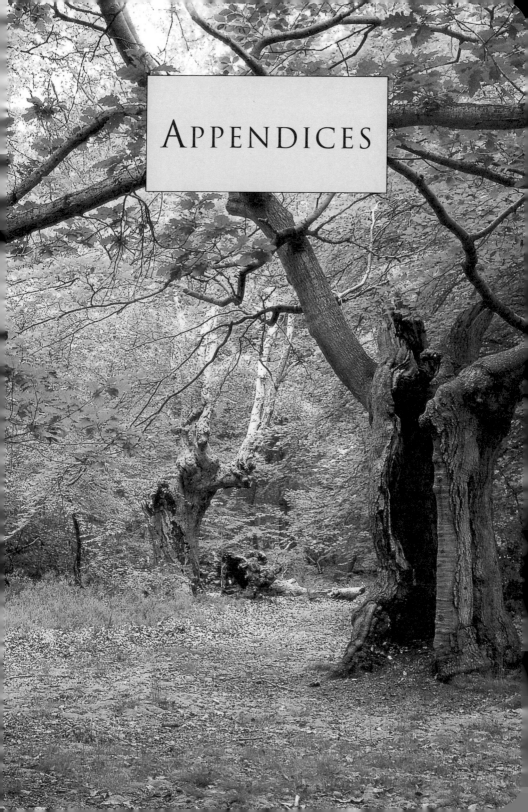

APPENDICES

GLOSSARY

Achene small, dry, hard, one-seed fruit that does not split open for seed distribution

Alternate to describe leaves that do not grow opposite each other

Angiosperm a term used to describe plants whose seeds are completely enclosed within an ovary, but more generally simply to mean a flowering plant

Anther part of the stamen that releases pollen

Aril coat that covers seed, often fleshy

Axil upper angle between a part of the plant and the stem that bears it

Axillary borne in an axil, usually referring to flowers

Bipinnate used to describe leaf arrangements in which the leaflets themselves are pinnate

Bract modified leaf at the base of a flower, flowerhead or seed

Buttress a root that supports a tree trunk

Calyx collective name for sepals, at base of flower below petals

Cambium a layer of cells within a tree trunk that generates new growth

Catkin a cylindrical cluster of male or female flowers

Chlorophyll the green colouring matter than enables photosynthesis

Chloroplast part of a tree cell that contains chlorophyll

Class a term used in Linnean classification to describe a large taxon (group)

Columnar a tree shape that is taller than broader with parallel sides

Compound used to describe a leaf that is divided into leaflets

Cone the seed-bearing structure of coniferous trees

Coniferous trees that bear cones

Cultivar a variety of plant produced and maintained in cultivation

Cymes branched inflorescence with each axis ending in a flower

Cuticle protective waxy coating on leaves

Deciduous a tree that loses its leaves and remains leafless for some months

Dioecious unisexual, describing trees that carry either male or female flowers but not both

Drupe a type of fruit consisting of one or several hard seeds (stones), surrounded by a fleshy outer covering

Elliptic to describe a leaf shape that is broadest in the centre, tapering at each end

Epidermis protective layer of cells on leaves and stalks

Evergreen a tree that bears leaves throughout the year

Family a term used in Linnean classification to describe a taxon (group) of middling-size, smaller than an order but larger than a genus

Genus a term used in Linnean classification to describe a small taxon (group), smaller than a family but larger than a species

Inflorescence a cluster of flowers

Lanceolate to describe a leaf that is broadest below the centre, tapering to the point

Leaflet the single division of a compound leaf

Lenticel a raised breathing pore on bark

Monoecious a tree with single-sex flowers but in which both sexes occur on the same tree

Native a species that occurs naturally in a particular region, as opposed to one that has been introduced

Needle a slender elongated leaf

Oblong to describe a leaf shape that is longer than broad, with parallel sides

Oblong-elliptic to describe a leaf shape that is oblong with rounded ends

Obovate to describe a leaf shape that is egg-shaped and broadest above the middle

Opposite to describe leaves that are borne in pairs on the opposite sides of an axis

Order in term used in Linnean classification to describe a taxon (group) smaller than a class and bigger than a family

Ovary the female flower part which contains the ovules which develop into seeds

Ovate to describe a leaf shape that is broadest below the middle

Palmeate a compound leaf that is divided into leaflets, arising from a single basal point

Panicle a head of stalked flowers

Petiole leaf-stalk

Phloem soft tissue within a tree trunk that transfers food around the tree

Pioneer species a species that is the first to colonize an area of ground, leading the way for other vegetation

Pinnate a compound leaf arrangement in which the leaflets are arranged alternately or in opposite pairs on a central axis

Pistil female reproductive organ of a flower

Pendent dangling

Pome an accessory fruit, such as an apple

Raceme inflorescence of stalked flowers radiating from a single, unbranched axis, with the youngest flowers near the tip

Sepal segment of a flower's outer whorl

Species in Linnean classification, the basic ranking of living creatures

Stamen the male part of a flower

Stigma the female part of a flower that receives pollen

Syncarps an aggregate or multiple frit, produced from fused pistils

Xylem woody tissue within the tree trunk that carries water and minerals

LEAF SHAPES

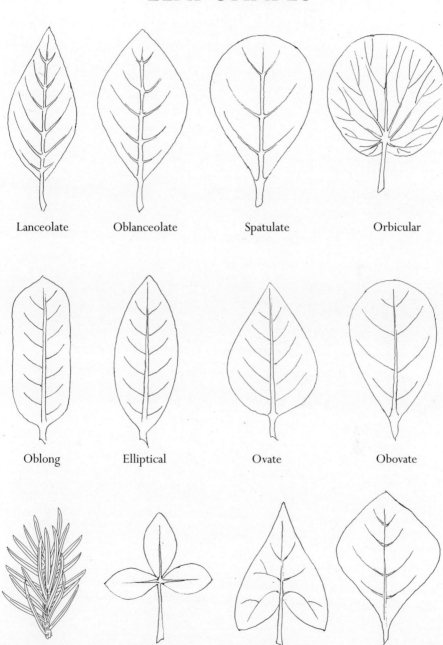

Lanceolate Oblanceolate Spatulate Orbicular

Oblong Elliptical Ovate Obovate

Needle Tripalmate Arrow-shaped Rhomboidal

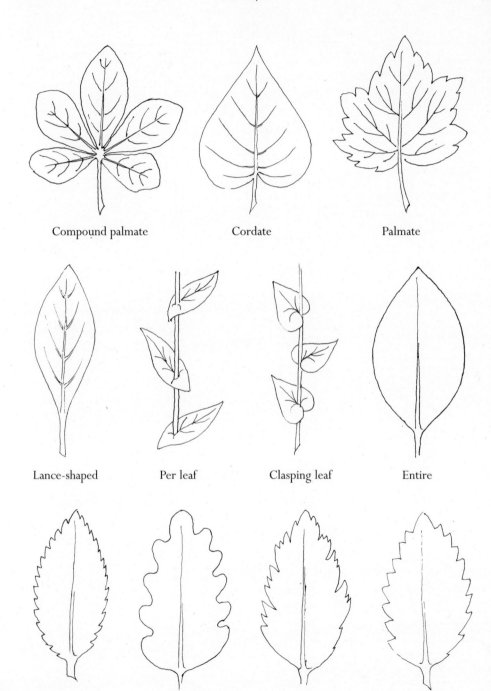

Compound palmate   Cordate   Palmate

Lance-shaped   Per leaf   Clasping leaf   Entire

Serrated   Lobed   Incised   Toothed

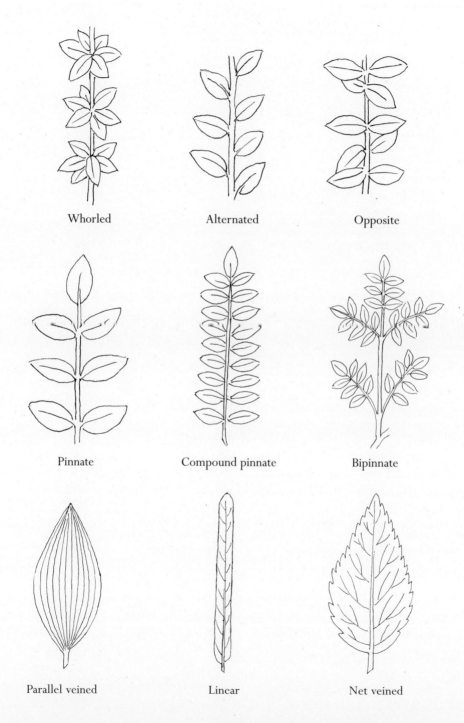

Whorled   Alternated   Opposite

Pinnate   Compound pinnate   Bipinnate

Parallel veined   Linear   Net veined

INDEX

BIBLIOGRAPHY

Davidson, Alan, Jaine, Tom (Ed),
The Oxford Companion to Food, (Oxford University Press, 2006)

Fitter, Alistair, *Gem Guide to Trees*, (HarperCollins, 2004)

Hora, Bayard (Ed), *The Oxford Encyclopedia of Trees of the World*,
(Oxford University Press, 1981)

Humphries, C.J., Press, J.R., Sutton, D.A.,
Guide to Trees of Britain and Europe, Hamlyn, 2000

Johnson, Owen & More, David,
Collins Tree Guide, (HarperCollins, 2004)

Pakenham, Thomas,
Remarkable Trees of the World, (Weidenfeld & Nicholson, 2002)

Press, Bob, *Trees of Britain and Ireland*, (HarperCollins, 1996)

Ridsdale, Colin, White, John, Usher, Carol,
Eyewitness Companions Trees, (Dorling Kindersley, 2005)

Russell, Tony & Cutler, Catherine,
The World Encyclopedia of Trees, (Anness Publishing, 2003)

Sutton, David, *Kingfisher Field Guide to the Trees of Britain and Europe*,
(Kingfisher Books, 1994)

Tudge, Colin, *The Secret Life of Trees*, (Penguin Books, 2006)

PICTURE CREDITS

The publisher would like to thank the following photographers and picture libraries for their kind permission to reproduce their images in this book.

Oxford Scientific Films:
OSF 80, 89; Botanica 204; Bower, Erwin & Peggy 70; Hendley, Ray 190; Ingram, Jason / Garden Picture Library 56; Kidd, Geoff 74,75; Mead, Ted 88;; Photononstop 121; Taylor, Harold 222,223; Winslow, Robert 54;

Corbis: 69, 72, 79, 92, 121, 155, 213, 219, 231

Ardea:
Ardea 24, 45, 59,76, 94, 116, 138, 140, 142, 144, 156, 165, 171, 172, 177, 182, 186, 192, 214, 232; Auscape/Densey Clyne 14, 96, 100, 118, 120; Bahr, Chris Martin 60, 201; Bevan, Brian 15; Bomford, Liz & Tony 209; Brunskill, Chris 216; Cancalosi, John 68; Clay, Mary 66, 234; Coster, Bill 13, 62; Daniels, John 20, 58; De Meester, Johan 5, 18, 38, 112; Dixon, David 7, 17, 19, 40, 46, 50, 150, 175; Dressler, Thomas 12, 108, 224; Ferrero, Jean Paul 237; Fink, Kenneth 168, 227, 114, 122, 129; Gibbons, Bob 1, 26, 41, 44, 55, 84, 98, 126, 132, 136, 152, 154, 158, 159, 160, 170, 174, 179, 228, 230, 238; Goetgheluck, Pascal 39; Gohier, Francis 42, 4352, 124; Hadden, Don 90; Knights, Chris 184; Labat, Jean Michel 148, 176; Laub, Jens-Peter 2, 9, 11, 32, 178, 188, 200, 202, 208, 240; Leeson, Tom & Pat 48; Lindau, Ake 23, 30/31, 134, 241,164, 7t; Lucas, Ken 109; Mason, John 3, 36, 65, 94, 101, 115, 149, 162, 193, 194; Morris, Pat 104, 180, 199, 218, 236; Paterson, Allen 29, 220, 226; Porter, Richard 210; Steyn, Peter 110, 196; Swedberg, John 206; Usher, Duncan 34, 146; Van Gruissen, Joanna 145, 166, 212, 242; Waller, Richard 4; Watson, M. 6, 78, 82, 86, 102, 130, 198, 211; Weisser, Wardene 64, 106, 107, 137

Getty Images:
245, 246, 248

Cover Images
Main Image:
English oak tree © Travelpix Ltd/Getty Image

Tiled images:
All © iStockphoto